crafts in plastics

NICHOLAS ROUKES

crafts in plastics

WATSON-GUPTILL PUBLICATIONS • NEW YORK

To Kathleen

First published in 1970 by Watson-Guptill Publications,
a division of Billboard Publications, Inc.
165 West 46 Street, New York, New York
All Rights Reserved.
No portion of the contents of this book may be reproduced or used
in any form or by any means without written permission of the publishers.
Manufactured in Japan.
ISBN 0-8230-1000-7
Library of Congress Catalog Card Number: 70-117075

Edited by Susan E. Meyer
Designed by James Craig
Composed in eleven and fourteen point Caledonia
by York Typesetting Co., Inc.
Printed by Toppan Printing Co., Ltd.

ACKNOWLEDGMENTS

The author wishes to express his thanks to Dr. Rodney Roche of the Polymer Chemistry Laboratory at The University of Calgary, Alberta, for technical suggestions; to the artists contributing photographs of their work for this publication; to the students in the author's classes at The University of Calgary who have contributed photographs of their work; and to Trudy Welsford for typing the manuscript. Special thanks to Donald Holden, editor of Watson-Guptill Publications, and to Susan E. Meyer for editorial assistance.

BIBLIOGRAPHY

Arnold, Lionel K., *Introduction to Plastics,* Iowa State University Press, 1968.

DeDani, A., *Glass Fiber Reinforced Plastics*, Interscience, New York, 1961.

Gutierrez, José, and Roukes, Nicholas, *Painting with Acrylics,* Watson-Guptill, New York, 1965.

Lawrence, J. R., *Polyester Resins*, Reinhold, New York.

Lee, H., and Neville, K., *Epoxy Resins, Their Application and Technology*, McGraw-Hill, New York, 1957.

Modern Plastics Encyclopdedia, McGraw-Hill, New York, 1967.

Moholy-Nagy, *Vision in Motion*, Paul Theobald, Chicago, 1947.

Newman, Thelma R., *Plastics As An Art Form*, Chilton, Philadelphia, 1964.

Oleesky, Samuel, and Mohr, Gilbert, *Handbook of Reinforced Plastics of the S.P.I.*, Reinhold, New York, 1964.

Percy, H. M., *New Materials in Sculpture*, Alex Tiranti, London, 1962.

Roukes, Nicholas, *Sculpture In Plastics*, Watson-Guptill, New York, 1968.

Seuphor, Michel, *The Sculpture of This Century,* George Braziller, New York, 1960.

Simonds, Herbert R., and Church, James M., *Concise Guide to Plastics*, Reinhold, New York, 1963.

Society of Plastics Industry, *Plastics Engineering Handbook* (Third Edition), New York, 1960.

Scientific American, Volume 217, Number 3, September, 1967 (Materials Issue).

". . . The World Crafts Council should develop its activity essentially with craftsmen who work in the context of the culture of our times, of that culture which takes into account the new socio-economic realities of modern man, abandoning once and for all the historical and traditional concepts which have relegated the craftsman to a phenomenon of custom, folklore, or art for the tourist. From such activity of the council there will come, as one of the results, a greater impulse in the search for new techniques, for the use of new materials, for the natural stimulus that is derived from the constant and systematic comparison of different methods of work and cultural attitudes . . ."

Mr. Nino Caruso, from a panel discussion at
The World Crafts Council, Montreux, Switzerland, 1966.

INTRODUCTION

Although polymer technology is one of the younger sciences, plastics play an important role in our day-to-day life. Engineers prophesy that tomorrow's builders may turn to polymeric materials almost exclusively, that medical science will rely heavily on polymeric chemistry for creating substitute vital organs, and that future trains, automobiles, aircraft, roadways, and even spacecraft may be made of polymeric substances. This, then, is the polymeric age—the exciting era of man-made materials, a period synonymous with the exploding cornucopia of gadgets and goods designed for creature comfort and the better life.

The art world also reflects the impact of synthetic materials. A visit to any contemporary gallery will reveal a great number of glistening, brightly colored paintings, sculptures, and constructions made from a variety of plastics. Beautifully designed lamps, chairs, jewelry, clothing, and household items made from plastics are now commonplace in craft centers around the world.

The artist is determined to push back traditional boundaries in his quest for new forms and expression, with the result that values in art—and even its very definition—have been challenged. "Art" has been transformed from noun to verb, calling for an attitude of involvement and encounter for both artist and spectator. More people than ever before participate in making art objects and collecting the works of contemporary artists and craftsmen.

Polymeric Materials

The term polymer is derived from Greek, meaning many parts. Polymers are complex molecular patterns, combinations of many blocks, or monomers, into long, flexible chains. Nature has created natural polymers for thousands of years; they are commonly found in such substances as wood cellulose and animal protein, and in milk, butter, wax, and silk products. Only recently, through the use of modern instruments such as electronic microscopes, centrifuges, and X-ray diffraction equipment, has man been able to probe, analyze, and extract the secrets of nature's polymeric structures. Using such raw materials as petroleum, coal, salt, air, and water, chemical engineers have been able to invent *synthetic* polymers—an event which should be heralded as one of the major contributions of our age. Today, polymer chemists have evolved many sophisticated combinations of synthetic polymeric chains which have yielded a vast array of plastic products.

Artistic Expression with Plastics

Traditional substances, such as wood, metal, stone, and glass, have basic inherent properties or "personalities" which almost dictate the means by which they can be formed and manipulated. Because their physical properties and surface characteristics are constant, the artist is confined to work within certain limitations.

Plastics differ, however, in that their basic structure must be created *first,* before the subsequent manipulation may take place; this allows the artist to tailor-make the physical characteristics of his material. He may choose to have his material hard or soft, flexible or rigid; optically clear, translucent, or opaque; integrally colored, textured, and of varying degrees of strength. Plastics offer the artist not one, but many means for artistic expression— all of which may be considered natural and honest.

Application of Plastics to Crafts

The plastics industry has a great number of materials to offer the adventuresome craftsman. Among these are the following:

(1) *Acrylics:* Water soluble emulsions, paints, gesso, and paste extenders are commercially obtainable through art stores. In solid form, acrylics are available in sheets, blocks, rods, and tubes, and range from transparent to translucent or opaque, in a complete spectrum of colors. Liquid acrylic, commonly referred to as acrylic monomer, methyl methacrylate monomer, is not commonly used by artists as yet, due to complex equipment and methods required to process it.

(2) *Polyester:* A great variety of liquid polyester resins are marketed by paint stores and boat shops. Polyester resins are non-water based materials, requiring a catalyst to polymerize, or harden, the plastic to a rigid state. They can be purchased in various forms, ranging from a thin honey-like to thick, vaseline-like consistency. Various types of resins include laminating polyester resin, surfacing resins, and clear casting polyester resins.

(3) *Epoxies:* These are produced as coatings, pastes, and adhesives. The resins—generally used as automobile body putties—exhibit an outstanding adhesiveness for joining many dissimilar materials, have a remarkable strength, and may be utilized as modeling putties. Two-system paints, involving epoxy paint and hardener, are stocked by most paint stores, and are unsurpassed for achieving brilliant, porcelain-like surfaces.

(4) *Vinyls:* These are manufactured in flexible sheets for vacuum forming, cutting, and constructing. Clear vinyl is used for making inflatable see-through furniture, and soft sculptural forms. Vinyl inks, used to silk screen on plastic surfaces, range from opaque to transparent. Sprayable

vinyl, for cocooning, requires special equipment, but may be used to create sculptural surfaces which are soft and flexible. Other thermoplastic sheeting suitable for craft use includes butyrate, polyethylene, polypropylene, polystyrene, ABS, and polyvinyl chloride.

(5) *Cellular Plastics:* These are expanded plastic "foams", such as polystyrene and polyurethane, which are commonly known by such trade names as Dow's Styrofoam and DuPont's DyPlast, generally distributed by hardware stores or building supply yards.

Although there are a great number of other plastics available, in this text we shall be concerned mainly with those mentioned above. A detailed description of various plastics and their properties may be found in a previous book by this author, *Sculpture in Plastics,* also published by Watson-Guptill Publications.

Two Basic Categories

Generally speaking, plastics may be grouped into two families—thermoplastic and thermosetting.

Thermoplastic resins must be softened by physical heat before they can be shaped. They will harden when cool, but will soften again if reheated. This group includes acrylics, vinyls, polyethylene, polystyrene, ABS, polypropylene, and the polyfluorocarbons.

Thermosetting resins are shaped by the application of either chemical or physical heat, but once formed will not resoften with the subsequent application of heat. Included in this latter category are the polyesters, epoxies, alkyds, acrylics, silicones, and caseins.

The Craftsman in the Twentieth Century

The need for expression with tools and materials is instinctive. Man is a creature possessing a natural drive to decorate not only himself, but his environment as well. Today, man's basic tools, his hands, have been "extended" through machines and complex devices. Although machines greatly facilitate his tasks, they tend to disassociate him from direct contact with materials. The mindlessness of machines isolates the spirit of man by threatening to dehumanize him. The professional craftsman and hobbyist seeks to maintain man's contact with his tools and media, thus helping to preserve an integrated idiom of man living in tune with technocracy.

The contemporary craftsman, unlike the guildsman of earlier years, is concerned with much more than hand skills and utilitarian function in the production of his wares. The need for personal involvement in the creation of art objects greatly increases while our society becomes more complex. As our lives become multi-dimensional, craft objects fulfill multi-functional needs—physical, psychological, spiritual, emotional, intellectual, educational, or recreational—serving all or part of these requirements and changing as our needs change.

The modern craftsman is an artist-designer. Knowledgeable in many products and processes, he seeks to go beyond the limiting attitude of doing "old things with new materials," to a more daring concept of creating "new things with new materials." In the opinion of Mrs. Armi Ratia, director of Finland's Marimekko Design Studios, the demands placed upon the twentieth century craftsman go even further than a mastery of technique and expression:

> To succeed as a crafts designer, the young artist of today must possess talent, taste, technique, tact, talk, tenacity, and timing. He is no longer a cloistered technician working in a dark isolated shop, but one who is knowledgeable and deeply involved with socio-economic issues of our times, and who seeks to serve the dynamically changing needs of our culture.

In basements, studios, and classrooms across the nation, there is an exploding interest and involvement with crafts. With the advent of even greater leisure time in the future, crafts will undoubtedly constitute an important avenue of personal expression, and a creative outlet for individual well-being. This book is intended to provide information, techniques, and processes not only for the professional craftsman, but also for the Sunday hobbyist and student eager to know more about the applications and possibilities of synthetic materials in the world of art.

Within the field of graphics, there are many areas in which plastics may be employed: as materials for making various types of printing plates; as printing surfaces; as special printing or screening inks; and as material capable of being thermoformed into a variety of dimensional "multiples."

Whether the artist is concerned with relief, intaglio, or stencil methods of printmaking, there are many plastic materials which may be used. A few of the methods which are well on their way to becoming standard practice within the graphics field are the following:

SYNTHETIC MATERIALS FOR PRINTMAKING

(1) *Relief Processes:* Preparing Masonite panels with acrylic gesso or modeling paste to create printmaking plates; making collograph plates with paper, cardboard, plastic, textured and loose materials, using acrylic emulsions and acrylic modeling paste; using expanded plastic—such as polystyrene or polyurethane—and incising lines with mechanical or heat tools to create printing plates.

(2) *Intaglio Processes:* Using thermoplastic sheets for making drypoint or engraved plates.

(3) *Stencil Processes:* Using polymer emulsions and mediums for silk screen blockout, plastic paints for screen printing.

(4) *Experimental "Multiples":* Use of thermoplastic materials and vacuum forming processes for making high relief multiples.

Acrylic paste extender may be applied to the surface of Masonite panels and will dry to produce a soft, easily carved surface. The surface can then be carved with tools, such as linoleum gouges, knives, nails, or other makeshift utensils. The surface is then inked in the traditional manner, wiped, and printed, using a typical etching press or hand baren.

To produce printing plates with acrylic modeling paste, it is particularly effective to completely cover the surface of Masonite with the paste, using a trowel or putty knife, and then to manipulate the material while it is still partially wet. Interesting textures may also be achieved by pressing a variety of textured materials or fabrics into the moist surface. Burlap, wire screen, wadded paper, and similar types of materials are suitable for this purpose.

By using small pieces of cardboard as squeegees, the paste may be further manipulated to achieve additional textures, forms, and lines. Very fine lines may be made by using a pencil, "drawing" directly into the moist paste, before it has had a chance to dry completely. Allow twenty-four hours for the prepared surface to dry, and then sand the surface slightly to remove sharp peaks. Then give the plate a liberal coat of acrylic polymer medium, and allow it to dry. The prepared Masonite panel is now ready for printing.

Regular oil base, offset lithography inks may be used, applied with a household brush, wiped with cheesecloth, and printed with an etching press. Printed without inking, the acrylic plates will produce high-relief embossed prints on dampened paper. The photographs and captions in this chapter describe the process in greater detail. Two-color effects may be achieved by first inking and wiping the plates, using the method described above, and then by lightly rolling the plate with a contrasting color, using a printing roller or brayer. The first color settles into the "valleys", while the second remains on the "peaks", and both are transferred to the paper in printing.

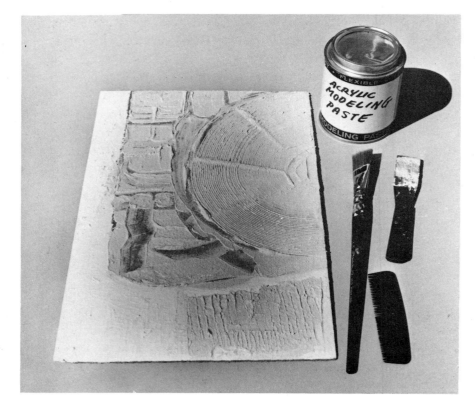

Step 1: Acrylic modeling paste is liberally applied over the surface of Masonite, and allowed to "set" partially, but not to dry completely. While in a semi-dry state, the surface is manipulated with a variety of tools, such as cardboard squeegees, combs, and wadded paper. The plate is allowed to dry, and sanded to remove peaks of the hardened paste extender which had formed.

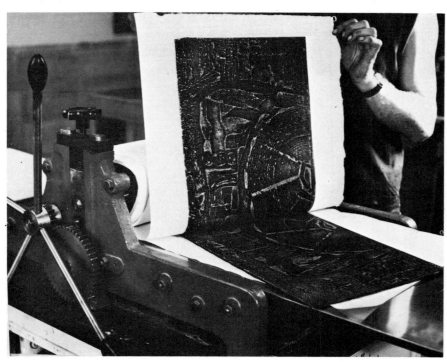

Step 2: The plate is inked, using commercially available offset lithography ink, applied with a stiff household brush. It is wiped by using a piece of gathered cheesecloth, wiping in semi-circular motions. The plate is printed with light pressure, using dampened Arches paper, on an etching press. A felt blanket placed over the surface of the paper equalized the pressure to insure evenness in the printing process.

Earth Structure, the completed print, by Nicholas Roukes, 15″ x 20″

Collography is a fairly recent innovation in printmaking, calling for the process of making "collage plates." These plates are usually fabricated by gluing paper shapes, textural materials, and other flat materials to a flat surface, usually cardboard or Masonite. The plate is then sealed with polymer medium, inked, and printed, usually with a roller type of press. Polymer emulsions, such as the matt or gloss medium made for acrylic painting, serve admirably as adhesives for attaching the various materials to the working surface. When the collage plate is dry, two to three coats of polymer medium are also applied over the entire surface to seal the porous materials and to provide a better surface for inking. The polymer medium should be thinned with equal parts of water and applied liberally over the surface with a flat brush.

Inking the collograph plates may be accomplished with a roller or brayer and oil base printing inks. Offset printing inks, available from local printers, are well suited for inking these plates. If the ink is extremely thick, it may be softened slightly by adding a few drops of lithographic varnish or a small amount of petroleum jelly. With experimentation, the artist can achieve many interesting effects by applying more than one color with the roller. Exercise considerable care in inking the collograph plates, since good results depend primarily on this operation. Many types of printing papers may be used for making collograph prints. Among those recommended are heavy, fairly soft cover stock; Arches or Rives papers. The paper should be dampened before printing. Good results are obtained by dampening both sides of the sheets of printing paper, placing them between sheets of moist blotter paper, and covering them with plastic or oil cloth. This sandwich is weighted with a flat board, and allowed to "damp" for a few hours—or preferably overnight. In printing collograph plates, a roller press or etching press—set at light pressure—is most effective. Place the dampened printing paper over the inked plate on the bed of the press, and cover this with a felt blanket. The plate is run through the press with an even motion, avoiding stopping over the plate. The collograph plates may be used many times, and cleaned in the conventional way, by using varsol, turpentine, paint thinner, or a similar mild solvent.

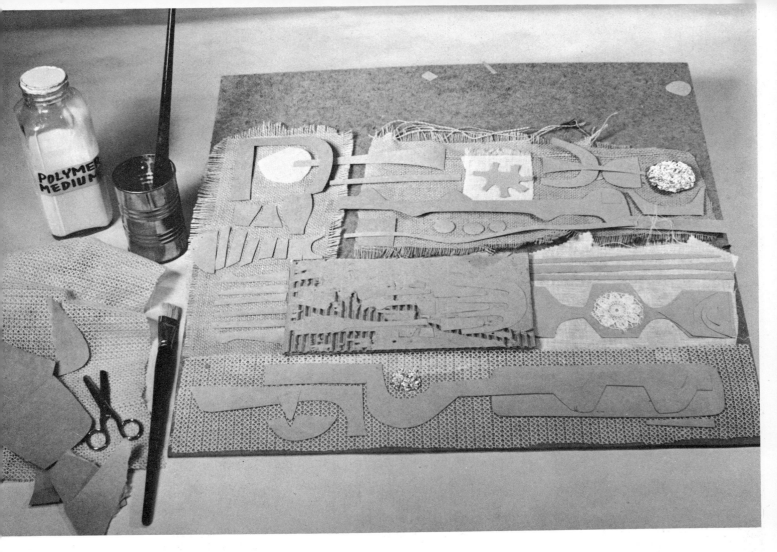

Step 1: (above) A variety of papers and fabrics are cut and arranged over a surface of Masonite. The shapes are shifted and rearranged until a desirable composition is achieved, and then these are attached to the surface with polymer medium or polyvinyl glue (Elmer's Glue).

Step 2: (left) Polymer medium is thinned with water, 1:1, and brushed liberally over the surface of the plate, thus sealing the porous materials and preparing the plate for inking.

21

Step 3: (above) Offset lithographic ink is rolled up on a glass slab and applied to the plate with a rubber roller. The ink is carefully applied, and rolled up in two colors before printing.

Step 4: (left) Dampened Arches paper is used for printing, and placed over the collographic plate. A felt blanket is carefully laid over the paper, and the etching press is set for light pressure.

Meta 1 (right) by Nicholas Roukes, 18″ x 30″. The final print is in two colors, black and sepia.

Expanded polystyrene is available from most building and supply yards, usually under the trade names of Styrofoam, made by Dow, or DyPlast, made by DuPont. This is a cellular plastic material, widely used for insulation, is usually blue or white. A 1″ thick slab of this material, cut to size, may be used for relief printing in the following manner.

Printing plates made of expanded polystyrene are made by depressing the soft material with makeshift tools, such as nails, pencils, or sticks. To create an incised design on this material, it is extremely effective to employ hot tools, such as electric soldering pencils, or woodburning tools. By "drawing" with the electric soldering pencil over the plastic material, clean, incised lines are easily achieved. Take care, however, to provide adequate ventilation when burning this material; the fumes are toxic.

Rigid expanded polyurethane is another material commonly used as insulation and may also be used for making relief plates. This material *should not be burned* with hot tools, however, because the fumes are extremely toxic. If polyurethane is used, abrasive hand tools should be employed, or the material should be carved with electric Dremel tools, equipped with a high speed cutter head.

As the surface of expanded polystyrene is adversely affected by solvents in many paints and inks, exercise care to choose a printing ink that will not dissolve the material. Oil based printing inks or water based acrylic paints are recommended. If acrylic paints are used for printing, a few drops of glycol should be added to retard drying time.

Thin rice papers are especially suitable for printing, and the printing itself may be effected with a spoon or baren.

Step 1: Using an electric soldering pencil, incised lines are easily burned into the soft plastic.

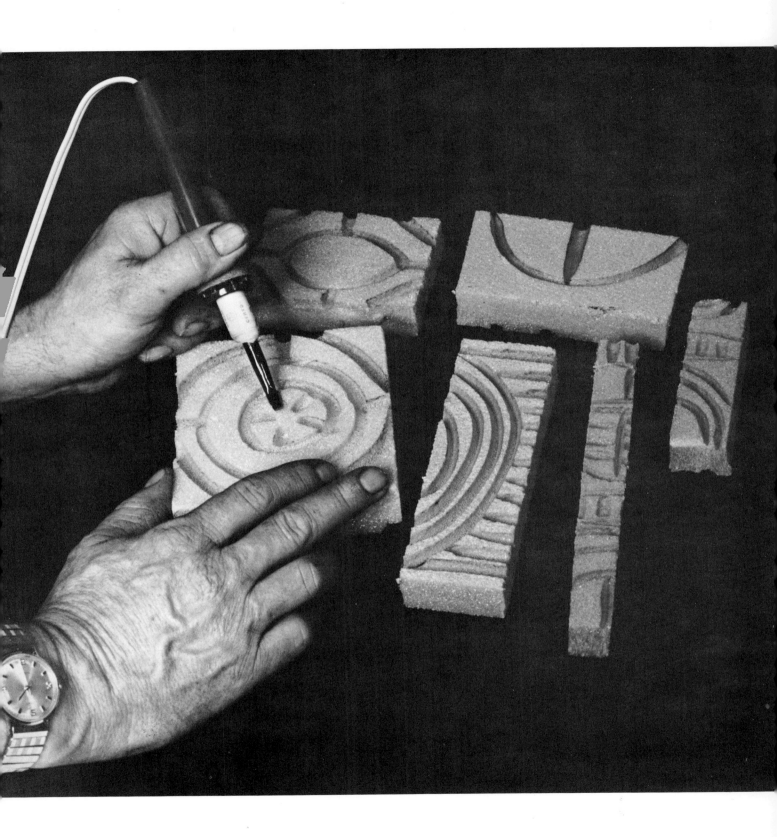

Step 2: (above) The polystyrene sections of the printing plate are assembled on a sheet of Masonite and attached using white glue. Oil based printer's ink was rolled up on a glass slab and applied with a rubber brayer.

Step 3: (right) No elaborate presses are required for this printing operation, and making many prints of consistent quality are possible from the plate. The characteristic texture of the expanded plastic is shown in this photograph. A lightweight oriental mulberry paper was used for making the print. The paper was placed over the inked polystyrene plate, and rubbed from the back with a large wooden spoon.

Thin sheets of acrylic plastic or other thermoplastic materials have soft surfaces which can easily be scratched or carved for intaglio printmaking.

Drypoint is a method of scratching the surface of a plate with sharp instruments, producing shallow furrows. These later catch the ink to effect printing. This process is similar to the traditional method of using drypoint—with copper or zinc plates—except that the softer thermoplastic is used as the plate. The plastic materials have the advantage of being transparent and, consequently, drawings or sketches may be taped to the underside of the material to act as a guide during the processing of the plate. Tools for drypoint may vary from makeshift scribers of steel, to sharpened dental tools, or professional carbide scribes.

Engraving is a method of employing tools such as burins, which actually remove a portion of the plastic, gouging out thin lineal channels deeper and crisper than drypoint lines.

In working with thermoplastic sheets for printmaking purposes, both drypoint and engraving techniques may be employed on a particular plate, depending on the effect that the artist seeks to create.

Inking the plate—in either the drypoint or engraving technique—is done in the traditional manner, by applying etching ink with a roller, brush, or tightly rolled piece of felt. Apply the ink over the entire surface of the plate with care, so that the engraved lines or furrows have been filled with ink. The surface of the plate is then carefully wiped clean, allowing the ink to remain in the channels only. For special effects, a thin film of ink may be allowed to remain on the surface of the plate, of course.

An advantage of the plastic plate is that the surface may be wiped absolutely clean for strong black and white contrasts. Tarlatan pads are excellent for wiping and are easily made by folding a few feet of tarlatan into a small pad. To remove surplus ink from the surface of the thermoplastic plate before wiping with the cloth pad, a small cardboard squeegee may be used. Final wiping may be done with the heel of the hand after using the pad. The edges of the acrylic plate should be beveled with a file before inking, so that they will not cut the felt blankets on the printing press.

Using an etching press which has been pre-adjusted to accommodate the thickness of the plastic plate, plus a couple of the usual felt blankets, place the inked plastic drypoint or engraving on the bed of the press, the dampened printing paper over it, and then two or three thin felt blankets over the paper. The bed is then rolled through the press, slowly and evenly, without stopping. Dry the proofs and prints flat by taping them to a piece of wood or drawing board and allow them to stretch tightly as they dry. Plastic plates are quite durable; they may be cleaned with mild solvents, and reused many times.

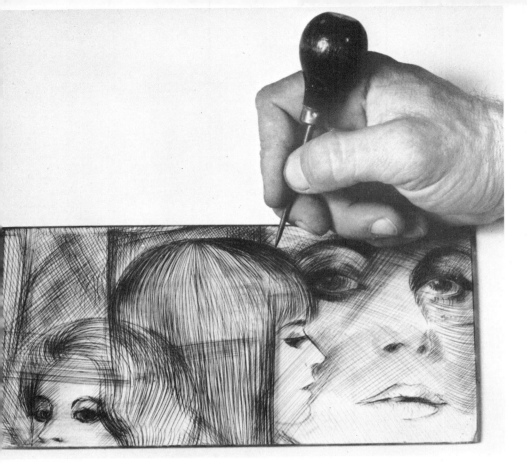

Step 1: Using a steel scriber, lines are scratched on the soft thermoplastic sheet. A preliminary drawing on paper may be taped to the underside of the plastic to act as a guide for the artist.

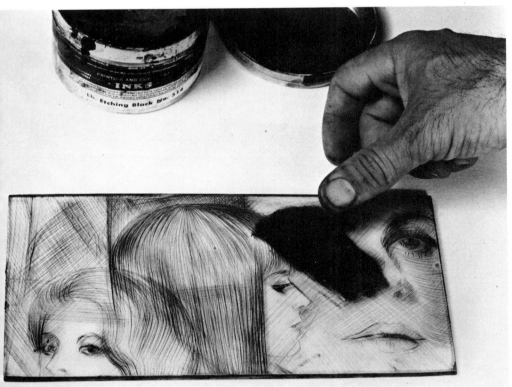

Step 2: The acrylic plate is inked with the thumb, acting as a dabber. Cover the entire plastic surface with etching ink, taking care to see that the ink is forced into the channels of the design. The surface of the plate is then wiped clean with a Tarlatan pad, followed with a final careful wiping with the heel of the hand. Care is taken not to remove ink in the furrows of the plastic plate.

Landscape (above) by Christopher Sayers, 5″ x 8″, dry point on acrylic.

Step 3: (left) An etching press is used to print the plastic plate. Dampened Arches paper is placed over the plate, followed with two felt blankets. The bed is rolled through the press with an even movement, without stopping.

An effective method of making plates for printing is to combine both intaglio (subtractive) means, and relief (additive) means, utilizing plastic materials.

In this project, the British printmaker, Shane Weare, is shown using a technique that he personally developed which incorporates these methods and materials.

As a basic surface, a sheet of 3/16″ acrylic plastic is used. Work is started by using an additive process. Various cut-out shapes of self-sticking vinyl plastic sheeting are applied to the plastic plate. These shapes are available in in a variety of patterns and textures from most building and supply houses. The sheet comes with a protective paper backing which is peeled from the back, and the pre-cut, sticky plastic forms are then pressed firmly to the acrylic base. By rubbing briskly with a soft cloth, the self-sticking forms are firmly attached to the working surface. By overlapping a variety of these texture films, interesting combinations of patterns may be created.

For lines and additional textures, the artist uses an intaglio technique, employing the use of sharp scribers and burins to carve the surface of the acrylic base sheet. The final plate is inked with etching ink, wiped, and printed with an etching press. The details of the process are shown in the ensuing photographs.

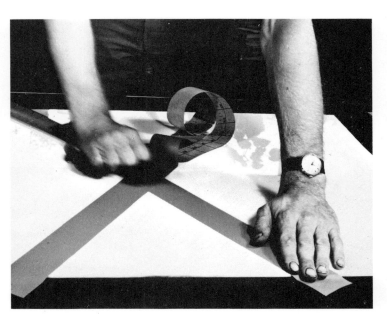

Step 1: The British printmaker, Shane Weare, begins work on his plate by carefully applying self-sticking vinyl sheeting to a flat surface of 3/16″ acrylic plastic.

Step 2: The patterned vinyl sheet is separated from a protective paper backing, placed carefully on the acrylic sheet, and then rubbed briskly with a soft cloth to firmly attach it to acrylic base.

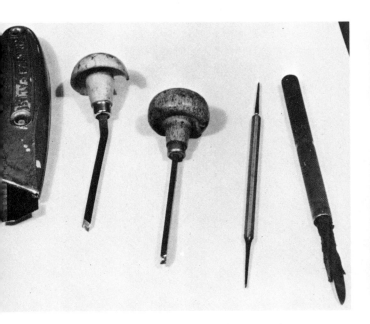

Step 3: Burins, and scribers are used to engrave and embelish the acrylic plastic sheet, tools capable of creating lines and additional textures on the plate.

Step 4: Additional shapes are cut from other patterned vinyl sheets, and intermediate forms and textures created by overlapping the self-sticking plastic sheets.

Step 5: A mat knife is used to cut intricate shapes from the self-sticking vinyl sheeting after it is applied to the surface of the plate. Sand, or other loose material, may also be sprinkled under the vinyl sheets for producing special textural effects.

Step 6: The edges of the acrylic plastic plate are beveled to prevent cutting the felt blankets of the etching press. The plate is now ready for inking.

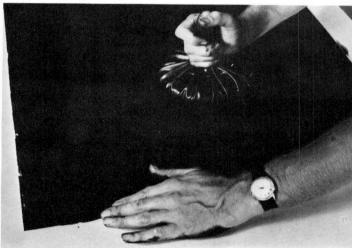

Step 7: Etching ink is applied liberally over the entire surface of the plate by means of a cardboard squeegee.

Step 8: A leather dabber is used to force the ink into the intricate surface patterns of the plastic plate. By rocking the dabber and covering the entire surface area, ink is forced into the minute details of the plate.

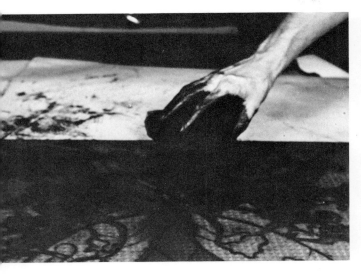

Step 9: A sheet of cheesecloth is wadded into a pad and used to wipe the plate. By using circular arc movements, the surface of the plate is gradually cleaned of the etching ink, allowing it to remain only in the recessed areas of the plate. For final cleaning, either the palm of the hand, or a clean sheet of paper is rubbed over the surface of the plate, removing the final film of ink from the surface of the plate.

Step 10: Shane Weare uses an etching press for the printing of his plate. Dampened Arches paper is placed face down over the inked plate, followed by two thin felt blankets, which are placed over the paper. The press, which has been pre-set to accommodate the thickness of the plate and the paper is set into a slow continuous movement, without stopping once the printing bed starts to move through the press.

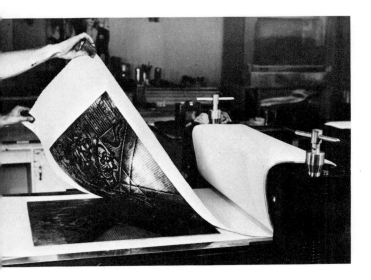

Step 11: The proof is lifted carefully from the plate.

Space Flowers (above), the final print, by Shane Weare, 24″ x 27″.

Eclipse (right) by Shane Weare, 22″ x 36″, intaglio and relief, utilizing acrylic and vinyl plastics for making the printing plate. The artist has used the same process described here.

The art of silk screening, or serigraphy, offers a great number of possibilities for the craftsman to explore standard or experimental means of incorporating synthetic media. Silk screening may involve synthetic inks for screening, synthetic materials for preparing the screen, or synthetic materials, such as plastics, for a printing surface.

Serigraphy is a stencil process of printmaking—a process of blocking out certain parts of a silk screen, either by the use of stencil films or stop-out liquids. In printing, a rubber squeegee is drawn over the silk, allowing ink to pass through the open areas.

There are advantages to using the silk screen process: no elaborate presses are required to make prints, and the artist has a certain mobility, because the screen may be moved over larger areas to create repeat design on rolls of fabric or transparent plastic.

There are many means of "blocking out" a silk screen. However, here we shall describe the use of *cutting film,* commonly known through its trade names of Profilm, Nufilm, Studnite, etc.

This stencil film is taped over a pencil sketch on a drawing board, and sections are then cut out and removed with an X-Acto knife. Take care not to cut all the way through the backing paper, which holds the remaining film in place. The completed stencil is attached to the silk with an adhering solution, and the backing paper is then peeled away. Butcher's tape is applied to the edges of the screen to block out the peripheral area which should not print.

There are a variety of synthetic inks available for silk screening.

Water based acrylic paints may be used, for example. However, they do present problems in clogging the screen on long runs, due to their inherent fast drying characteristics. Therefore, for silk screening purposes, a retarder, such as glycol or water wax extender, should be added to the acrylic paints.

Non-water based synthetic inks, available from sign shops or their suppliers, have more practical advantages for the craftsman. These may be used for long runs on a variety of materials, including transparent plastics. Some of these inks include *synthetic gloss enamels, vinyl inks, lacquer based inks, epoxy inks,* and *flexible plastisol inks.*

Some of the lacquer based inks are specially formulated to withstand the heat involved in vacuum forming, and are ideally suited for this purpose. Epoxy inks are formulated for tough problems and materials, and employ a catalyst which gives the ink a pot life of from five to eight hours. Some of the epoxy inks are labeled "baking epoxies," requiring 250°-300° heat for twenty to sixty minutes in order to effect a hard, porcelain-like surface. Plastisol inks are used for printing on fabrics, where an elastic-like coating is required. *Transparent bases* are available for many of these inks, in order to achieve translucent and transparent effects.

It should be mentioned that some of the solvents in the synthetic inks will adversely affect the cutting films, and the artist should first check to employ the correct film and block-out solutions recommended by ink manufacturers. (See Sources of Supplies.)

The water based polymer emulsion, or matt medium, may be painted directly on the silk as a stop-out medium, and can be used successfully with the water based acrylic paints or some of the non-water based screening inks. Of course, the traditional methods of employing animal glue, or the combination of animal glue-tusche are quite suitable for use with non-aqueous synthetic inks. Also, the photographic films, which are made of light hardened gelatin, are quite suitable for use with synthetic inks.

Step 1: Profilm is taped over a preliminary drawing. Areas of the profilm are cut and removed with an X-acto knife. Take care not to cut through the backing paper holding the remaining profilm in place.

Step 2: (left) Adhering the film to the silk screen. The screen is placed directly over the film and a soft cloth, saturated with film solvent, is rubbed over the surface, thus attaching the film to the silk.

Step 3: (above) The protective backing paper is peeled off. Butcher's tape is used on the edges of the screen to mask the peripheral edges.

Step 4: (above) Acrylic paint, with glycol retarder is used as a screening ink. The thick paint is forced through the open mesh of the silk with a rubber squeegee. Although there are advantages to using the water based acrylic paint as a screening ink, be careful to prevent the screen from clogging as a result of the normal fast drying characteristics of the medium.

Silk Screen on Paper (left) by Nicholas Roukes. The final print measures 16″ x 16″.

Silk Screen on Fabric (right) Using the same screen, acrylic paint was printed on fabric, demonstrating further possibilities of acrylic silk screening. There are many nonwater based synthetic inks which are specially formulated for textile printing. (See Sources of Supplies, textile inks for silk screening.)

Presensitized screen process films—which work somewhat like photographic film—for use in silk screening are commonly available from most drafting and art supply stores. They are commonly sold under many trade names, such as Ulano's prep or super prep, and Hi-Fi green prep film. Each film has an accompanying developer, usually available in two components, which is used to process the film after exposure.

Generally the artist first creates a drawing on a sheet of acetate plastic, using black acetate ink, and then places the drawing over the light sensitive photographic film. A glass plate is placed over these to press down and establish proper contact, and the exposure is made with incandescent or carbon arc lights. The exposure may be carried out in ordinary room illumination and usually varies from three to thirty minutes, depending on the particular type of film used and the strength of the light source. Test exposures should be made, in order to establish proper exposure time.

After the exposure is completed, the film is processed in a tray containing the prescribed developer. The film is then removed from the developing tray and subjected to a lukewarm spray of water (110°-115° F.) which is sprayed over the surface until all the negative areas of the film wash clear. To set the film, place it in a tray of cold water, and adhere it to silk, nylon, dacron, or wire screen, by placing the dampened film under the fabric and applying light blotting pressure with a small pad of newsprint paper.

Once dry, the plastic backing of the film is peeled away from the back of the silk screen frame. The edges are masked with butcher's tape and the prepared screen is now ready for printing. Most inks, except for water soluble inks, may be used for screening. Film may be removed with warm water or an enzyme remover, followed by a final cleaning with vinegar.

In the photographic section which follows, the Canadian artist, John Esler, utilizes presensitized process film in preparing his screen, and prints on Plexiglas acrylic sheet.

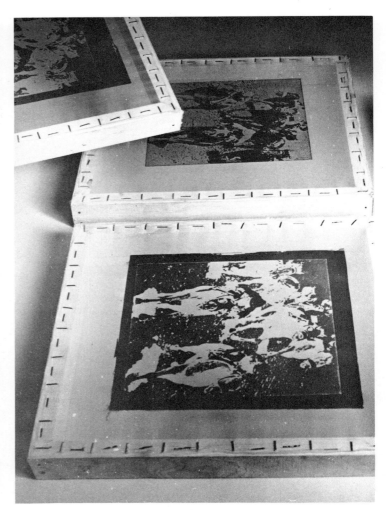

Step 1: John Esler used a discarded zinc engraving to make a print on white paper. He then gave the engraving to a local photo-engraver to make two negatives—one with a positive image and another with a reverse, negative image. These negatives were placed on presensitized screen process film which was exposed to a photoflood lamp. (In this instance, the exposure was for three minutes.) A sheet of plate glass was used to hold the negative in place while the exposure was being made.

Step 2: The processed presensitized film was attached to the silk with water and a soft pad of newsprint paper. Butcher's tape was used to mask out the outer edges of the silk screen frame prior to printing.

Step 3: (above) Using vinyl inks, the images were printed many times to develop the motif. Plexiglas acrylic sheeting, ¼″, was used as the printing surface. Before printing, the plastic was cleaned with an anti-static agent.

The Great Race (right) by John Esler, 36″ x 48″. The artist printed on both sides of the acrylic sheet, using black, white, and silver vinyl silk screen inks.

Diamond (above) by Audrey Capel Doray, silk screen on plastic. Images were drawn by hand, copied from news and advertising media, with Letratone dots overlayed. A photostencil was used to prepare the silk screen for printing. Prints were made using black, silver, and red vinyl inks on Mylar plastic.

French Money (left) by Larry Rivers, 30″ x 32″. Silk screen and collage. Eleven colors were screened on 100% rag board. Graphite gray was screened on ⅛″ Plexiglas, and ten Plexiglas cutouts were affixed to the surface of the board.

Printmakers today have broadened their attitudes in defining the contemporary graphic processes. The graphic artist has been influenced by the feedback from the ever-widening disciplines of modern painting and sculpture to accept experimental and mixed media approaches to his craft. The word *print* is often inadequate to describe contemporary experimental works—especially those involving three dimensional graphic work. Thus, the term *multiple* is used—defining works which are three dimensional, of a constructive nature, and often employ several media.

In this project, I shall describe a combined process of silk screening *and* vacuum forming. This method was used to produce a limited edition of twenty-five graphic multiples, entitled *Optos 25,* which exploit the transparency and optical characteristics of plastics. There are two components to this multiple: a transparent, vacuum-formed plastic relief which possesses lens characteristics, and a silk screen print of brilliant stripes, which is placed under the transparent relief to create shimmering effects which constantly change as the spectator moves in viewing the work. (For further instructions on vacuum forming, see Project 24.)

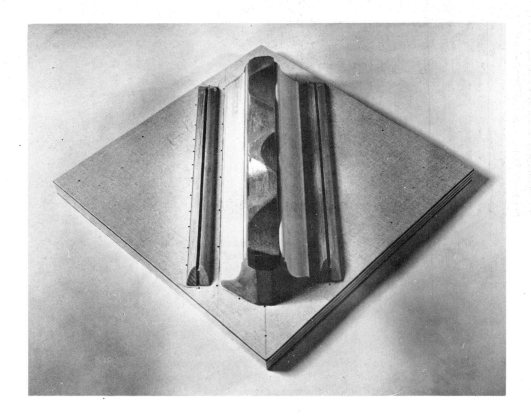

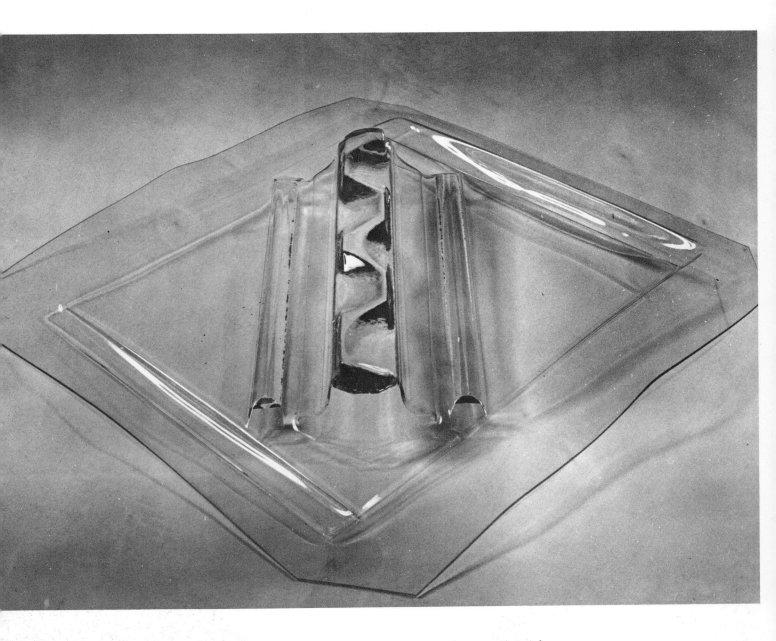

Step 1: (left) A wooden pattern is made for vacuum forming by using a variety of molding and picture frame materials. These components are carefully cut and assembled on a base of formica. They are glued to the base with an epoxy adhesive. Vacuum holes are drilled into the base approximately 1″ apart, using a 1/16″ drill bit.

Step 2: (above) The wooden pattern was placed on a vacuum forming machine and a plastic relief made by heating and vacuum forming a ⅛″ butyrate sheet over its surface. (The vacuum forming technique is described in detail in Project 24.) The formed plastic is given optical characteristics by pouring catalyzed clear polyester casting resin into the three cells.

Step 3: (left) Bold stripes of brilliant colors were silk screened on white illustration board, making the second component of this multiple.

Optos 25 (right) by Nicholas Roukes. Silk screen and vacuum formed plastic relief. (See plate in color section on page 120.)

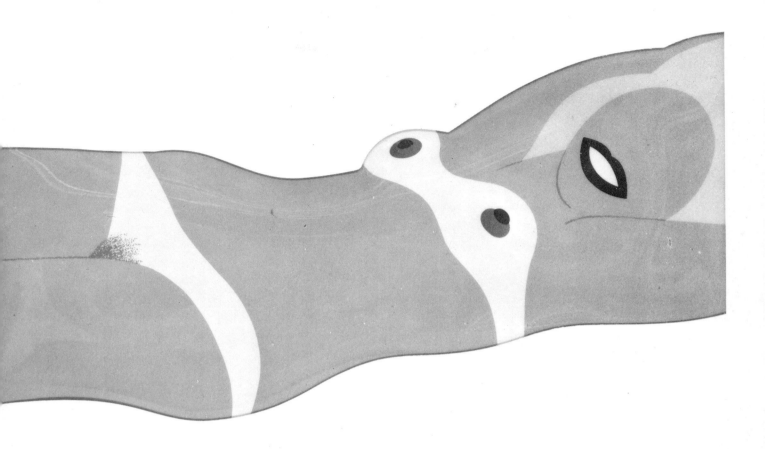

Cut Out Nude (above) by Tom Wesselmann, 7⅞" x 16¼", serigraph on vacuum-formed plastic. Collection, The Museum of Modern Art, New York.

Sixer (left) by Nicholas Roukes, 18" x 18", vacuum formed plastic over silk screen. This edition involved the construction of twenty-five multiples.

TEXTILE DESIGN

Water based acrylic paints have many applications within the realm of textile design. Designs may be painted directly, stenciled, block printed, or silk screened onto a variety of fabrics using the quick drying polymer paints. The acrylics dry hard and are water resistant, features which lend themselves admirably to the area of textile decoration. Furthermore, acrylics require no final fixing, as most textile dyes do. The artist will find that a few drops of glycol retarder added to the paints will prolong the working time appreciably.

The intense hues of many of the acrylic paints offer the artist an opportunity to thin the colors to a watery consistency and to paint directly on the fabric without losing color saturation. By using a variety of brushes and strokes, many effects may be created. Further control may be achieved by painting with wet-in-wet or drybrush techniques, applying the paint with sponges, rollers, or dripping, spraying, or spattering the paint onto the fabric.

In this section, the following methods of using acrylic paints for textile design are demonstrated:

(1) Stenciling with acrylic paint.

(2) Block printing with rigid polyurethane and acrylic paints.

(3) Silk screening on fabric with acrylics.

(4) Acrylic batik, a method of using acrylic paint and water wax extender.

Craft items, such as wall hangings, table settings, and articles of clothing, may be decorated by a variety of stencil techniques. An X-acto knife or a sharp mat knife may be used to cut stencil plates made of wax paper, cardboard, or thin plastic. Stencil brushes, especially designed for applying color through a stencil, are commercially available from most art supply stores. However, brushes used for painting—such as nylon or bristle types—are quite adequate for stenciling. The brushes should be charged with acrylic paint and then dabbed on a paper towel to remove surplus paint and moisture before applying the paint to the fabric. Brushwork should progress from the outside of the stencil towards the center, applying fairly light pressure and successive strokes in order to produce the proper shading and depth of color.

The fabric to be decorated should first be washed and ironed to remove sizing, and then stretched over a drawing board prior to printing. A few pieces of newsprint paper or a blotter under the material will serve to absorb excess color which may seep through the fabric. A separate brush should be used for each color, thus eliminating the need for frequent washing and subsequent softening of the stencil brushes, since the bristles are most effective when stiff.

Simple motifs may be repeated many times and overlapped to develop complex over-all designs and patterns. Even with a fairly heavy application of acrylic paint, the material remains pliable due to the flexible nature of the plastic base paints. The wall hanging shown in this project was created with bright red, yellow, and blue acrylics and measures 20" x 30".

Step 1: Stencil plates are cut from wax stencil paper in preparation for the creation of a decorative wall hanging. An X-acto knife and circle cutter are employed to create the stencils for this particular design.

Step 2: Linen is prepared by washing and ironing, and is then stretched over a drawing board. Acrylic paint, with a few drops of glycol added to prolong the working time, is drybrushed over the stencil. Use many light strokes, carefully working the color into the weave of the fabric and building the desired tonality and depth of color.

Step 3: (above) Designs are repeated and overlapped to create the composition. Blended or shaded effects are achieved by heavier applications of color.

Final wall hanging (right) 20″ x 30″, created with brilliant red, yellow, and blue acrylic paint on a linen fabric of light gray color.

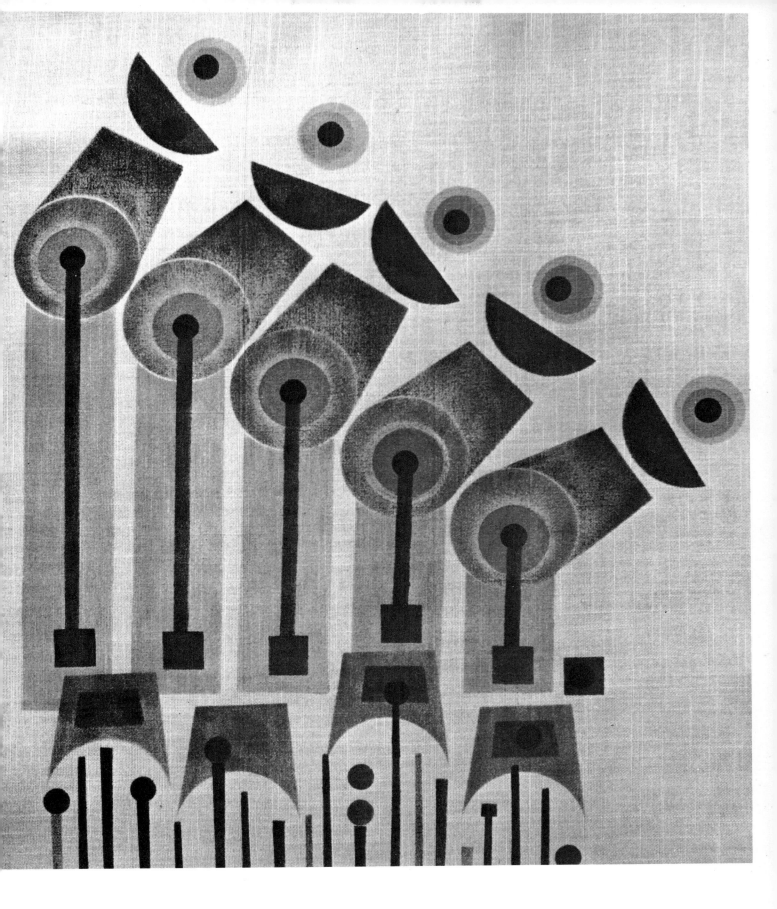

Rigid polyurethane, the lightweight expanded plastic commonly used for insulation, makes an ideal material for making printing blocks. The lightweight blue polystyrene slabs, common known by their trade names of Styrofoam or DyPlast, may also be used. The plastic materials are easily shaped with ordinary household tools, such as hacksaw blades, gouges, or kitchen knives. Shallow designs may be burned into the polystyrene material with electric soldering guns. The urethane, however, should not be burned, because this creates a noxious gas.

After washing and ironing the textile, acrylic paint is applied directly to the printing blocks with a flat bristle brush, and the printing is accomplished by using light hand pressure.

In the photographic demonstration of this project, three printing blocks were carved from polyurethane and printed with several colors to produce a design which was repeated many times over the surface of the fabric. The blocks were painted and printed each time until the entire surface of the cloth was covered in a checkerboard design. Variations in printing may be accomplished by dampening the cloth surface with a moist sponge prior to printing, a technique that produces softer edged forms. Further variations are achieved by using lighter fabric and printing on both sides.

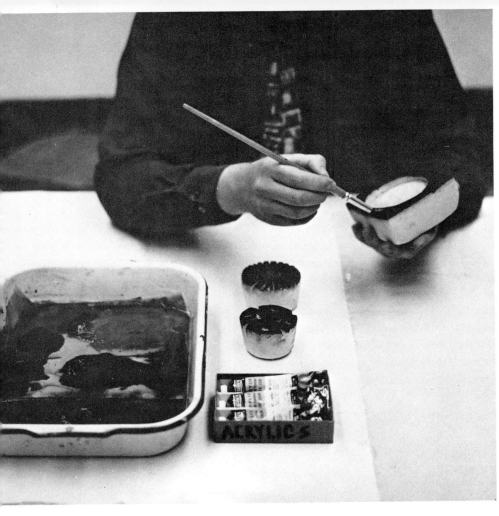

Step 1: Polyurethane blocks are carved to make printing stamps. These cellular plastic blocks are easily carved with knives, files, or sawblades. In this photograph, three blocks are shown which were carved to create a unit for printing an all-over design on fabric.

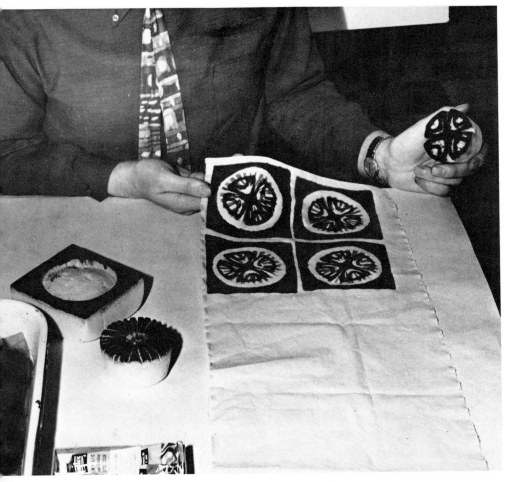

Step 2: Acrylic paint is brushed on to the surface of the urethane printing blocks with a bristle brush in preparation for printing. Light hand pressure is all that is required to print, and the blocks may be used many times. A few drops of glycol is added to the acrylic paint to extend drying time.

Summer dress printed with acrylic paint, using urethane blocks, by a first-year design student in the author's class. The fabric maintains its flexibility as a result of the flexible nature of the plastic paints, and does not require final fixing of colors, as they dry waterproof.

Styrofoam block print This photograph shows the effect of printing high density Styrofoam printing blocks on wet fabric, to produce controlled bleeding of color. Printing on both sides of the material creates a depth of color. Courtesy, Durable Arts, San Raphael, California.

The practice of silk screening acrylic paints is not generally recommended, because of the inherent fast-drying properties of the polymer base paints. However, successful results may be achieved by using coarser silk, such as 14XX grade for the screen, and by modifying the acrylic paint with a special retarding agent or extender. A few drops of glycol added to the paint will slow the drying time considerably, but it is suggested that the artist employ the more effective *water wax extender* created especially for this purpose. Water wax extenders are available from the Durable Arts Company in San Raphael, California (see Sources of Supplies).

In preparing a new silk screen, it is a good idea to scrub the surface of the screen with a kitchen cleanser and water (in order to remove sizing and oil spots) before cutting films are attached to the surface. Any of the traditional methods of creating stencil designs for silk screening may be employed as long as non-water based cutting films and block-out solutions are used. Before starting to print on the textile, screen a sample piece of cloth in order to check the color and technical printing qualities of the screen.

A good printing table may be made by using a sheet of ¾" plywood covered with a ⅜" felt underpad and two sheets of muslin cloth tacked over this surface. For smaller projects, a drawing board with several sheets of newsprint paper tacked to the surface should suffice.

Cloth to be screened should be thoroughly washed, ironed, and tacked to the surface of the worktable.

For professional results on larger projects, use a non-water based synthetic, ink such as Nazdar's series 6000 textile ink, which is especially formulated for silk screening on any type of textile material. This ink can be used with practically any type of stencil, including water soluble cutting films and the photo prep films.

Step 1: A lacquer-base cutting film is taped directly over a design and a stencil is cut with a sharp X-acto knife. As the shapes of the design are cut, they are removed from the wax backing.

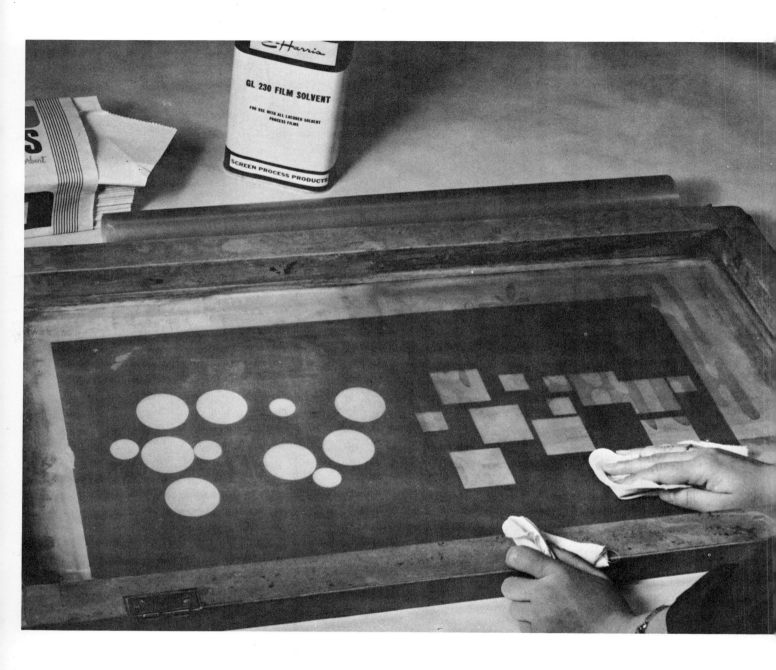

Step 2: The cutting film is attached to 14XX grade silk with the prescribed film adhering solution. The wax backing is then carefully peeled away from the silk, and the edges of the silk screen frame blocked out with butcher's tape.

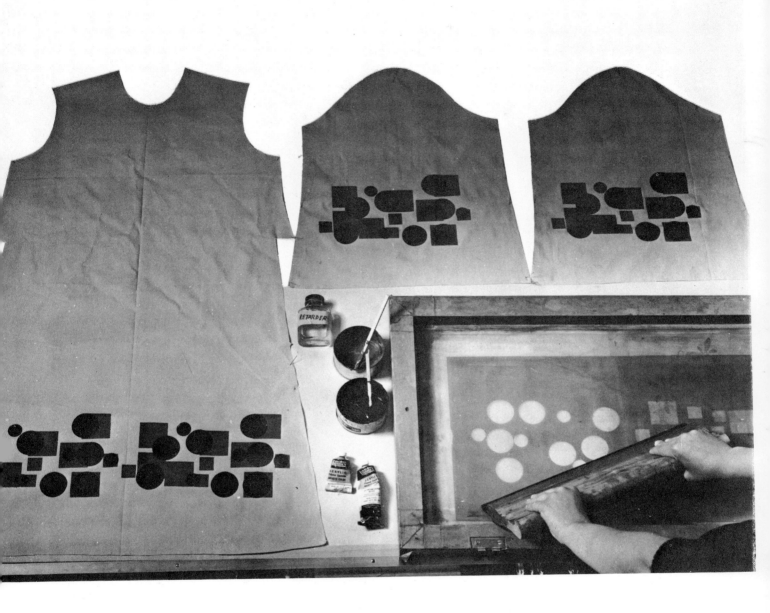

Step 3: A dress pattern is cut from lightweight linen and pinned to a work surface in preparation for printing. Glycol retarder is added to acrylic paint and squeegeed through the screen to produce a geometric design which runs along the bottom of the dress and along the bell sleeves.

Completed Dress (above) This simple, yet effective dress design was silk screened with bright blue and red acrylic paints on light blue linen.

Beach Ensemble (right) The smart outfit shown here was created by silk screening acrylic paint to a denim. Bright red and blue paint was printed on material of bright yellow.

PROJECT 12 ACRYLIC BATIK

The term *batik*, derived from the Javanese, refers to the art of drawing and painting designs on textiles with hot paraffin-beeswax mixtures, and subsequently dying the fabric. The procedure constitutes a resist, or block-out method of decorating textiles, since the dye adheres only to the areas not "blocked out" by the wax. Wax is removed from the cloth with hot water, with solvents, or by ironing, and the entire process of applying the wax and dyeing is repeated until the desired results are achieved.

In using acrylic paints for making batiks, either hot melted wax, or cold water wax emulsions may be employed as the resist medium. If the artist chooses to use hot wax as the resist medium, both paraffin and beeswax should be employed, blending the two waxes in a double boiler at a proportion of about 1:1. Note that hot waxes present potential fire hazards, and exercise great care to avoid overheating or direct exposure of the wax to flame. Paraffin wax melts at approximately 176°F., and beeswax at about 140°F. The waxes should be melted in a double boiler or similar device, and then may be applied to the fabric in many ways: with a spoon or ladle; brushes; hand-made stamps of wood, metal, or plastics; or by using the traditional tjanting tool which contains a reservoir for wax and a pipette for trailing fine lines.

To remove the paraffin-beeswax from an acrylic batik, place the batik between several sheets of newspapers, use an electric iron, and change the papers several times as you iron until the wax is absorbed.

Cold wax emulsions require no heat, and are safe, non-toxic materials which are quite suitable for use in classroom situations. A good water wax emulsion is available from Durable Arts Co., (called Cold Batik Wax), San Raphael, California (see Sources of Supplies).

Water wax emulsions, which have been prepared for use as extenders for acrylic paints or for use in making acrylic batiks, have a thick viscosity similar to heavy cold cream. They are completely water soluble and may be applied to fabrics with brushes, palette knives, small cardboard squeegees, or with the fingers. Precisely controlled patterns may be achieved.

Once the water wax has dried on the surface of the fabric, acrylic paints, synthetic textile pigments, or cold dyes—which have been thinned with water to a proportion of about 1:1—may be brushed or applied with a plastic foam roller over the surface of the cloth. Tacking the fabric to a wooden frame will help keep the cloth stretched during the painting operation.

Water wax may be removed from cloth by rinsing the fabric in lukewarm water and rubbing the surface gently until the wax falls away. The waxing and painting process is then repeated until the desired design results are achieved.

Step 1: Cold water wax extender may be applied with a brush, painting knife, or finger. For best results it should be quite thick.

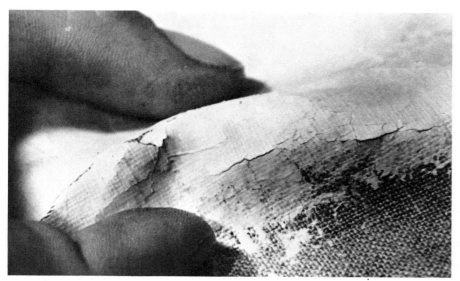

Step 2: After cold water wax is completely dried it may be cracked by wrinkling the fabric in a random pattern, or by deliberately introducing a designed crack pattern.

Step 3: Acrylic paints, textile pigments, or cold dyes are best applied with a plastic foam roller, but may also be brushed on. Colors should be quite liquid.

Step 1: A mixture of paraffin wax and beeswax is blended in a double boiler to create the block-out medium. The hot wax is applied to the fabric with brush, hand stamps, or the traditional tjanting tool. The textile to be decorated is stretched to a wooden frame.

Step 2: Hot wax is applied to the fabric with a brush to create the resist design. Manipulation of the fabric prior to dyeing creates a controlled cracking of the wax, imparting a rich textural quality to the acrylic batiks.

Step 3: Paraffin-beeswax resist is removed from the fabric by ironing the batik between sheets of newspaper. The papers are changed several times as the wax is absorbed.

Acrylic Batik (right) 22″ x 30″. Acrylic paints, thinned with water to a proportion of 1:1 were brushed over the material to produce the resist design.

In recent years, artists have found extensive use for plastics as a medium for making decorative objects in the home. In this section, we will examine some of the possibilities available to the artist.

ARCHITECTURAL AND INTERIOR DESIGN

Liquid Plastics for Interior Design

Polyester resin is a thermosetting plastic, available from most building supply houses, boat shops, or craft supply stores. This two-component system involves the use of a plastic resin plus a catalyst, which is added in very small quantities in order to transform the plastic from a liquid to a solid state.

The 'pot life" of polyester resin—i.e., the amount of time the resin remains liquid after the catalyst has been added—is determined by the amount of catalyst added, the ambient temperature, and the thickness of the pour. A few preliminary experiments will help determine the exact proportion of catalyst to resin but, generally speaking, a proportion four to six drops of catalyst per ounce of polyester resin is used for pours not exceeding ½″ thickness. Less catalyst is added for thicker pours. Massive forms may be built up by casting the resin in layers. This method avoids the excessive exothermic heat reaction and danger of fracturing which occurs with voluminous pours.

For more complete information regarding the nature of polyester resins, the reader should refer to my previous book, *Sculpture in Plastics.*

Safety Precautions

The polyester resins, catalysts, and thinners used for cleanup, are potentially hazardous to health, and should be employed with extreme caution. Avoid the toxic vapors and fumes, and exercise the following safety precautions at all times:

(1) *Ventilation:* Allow for plenty of ventilation, either by working in a properly vented studio, or outdoors. Chemical masks or extractors are recommended. Breathe only fresh air while working with these chemicals, as vapors have been known to cause dematitis, dizziness, and health problems of a more serious nature.

(2) *Handling Polyester Resins and Accessory Chemicals:* Avoid handling any of these chemicals directly. Disposable gloves should be employed, and throw away contaminated containers or used papers.

(3) *Catalysts:* Catalysts such as M.E.K. peroxide are toxic, flammable, and potentially explosive if subjected to severe shocks or falls. Avoid skin contact with this chemical and keep it away from heat or flame.

(4) *Cleanup Thinners:* Acetone and lacquer thinners are normally used for general studio cleanup when polyester resins have been used. Of the two, a good grade of lacquer thinner is preferable, thus avoiding the more hazardous acetone, which has an extremely low flash point. Skin contact and vapors from these thinners should also be avoided.

Do not smoke or eat while working with any of the above-mentioned materials. Polyester resins should never be stored in a refrigerator or container utilized for food storage.

In this section, three methods of using liquid plastics for interior and architectural design will be described:

(1) Making a window hanging of polyester resin.
(2) Making a translucent wall relief of polyester.
(3) Stained glass and plastic for architectural design.

Lamps from plastics

Plastics are also ideally suited for the creation of varied forms of lamp design. When designing lamps, the craftsman must consider utilitarian function, esthetic character, structural form and choice of materials, light source, appropriate luminosity, color filtration, and environmental effects. Within the realm of plastics, there are many materials to choose from that satisfy design requirements, such as strength, heat resistance, color transparency, and ease of forming, cutting, and assembling.

Several means of making lamps may be realized in a typical studio set-up without using elaborate or expensive tools and equipment. Plastics such as polyesters and acrylics are perhaps most commonly used by studio craftsmen for lamp design. Ordinary saws and shop tools may be used for forming acrylics, and no specific hazards are involved in working with this non-toxic plastic. Polyester resins, however, are toxic materials and provisions for ventilation should be considered, as has already been described.

In this section, three methods of using plastics for lamp design will be described:

(1) Making lamps with polyester paste over hump molds.

(2) Making tubular lamps with fibreglass cloth and polyester resin.

(3) Making lamps by blow-forming and decorating acrylic plastic.

PROJECT 13
MAKING A WINDOW HANGING FROM POLYESTER RESIN

In the method of making window hangings shown here, a ½" piece of plywood was cut with a sabre saw to create a variety of cells which were subsequently filled with liquid polyester resin. However, a cellular frame may also be made from welded or pierced metal, or from ceramic.

A thin sheet of Mylar plastic (DuPont polyester sheeting) was rubber cemented to the bottom of the cellular frame. In two pours, each cell was partially filled with catalyzed liquid polyester resin to which colored dyes had been added. As resin changes from a liquid to a solid state, it passes through a gel state. In this project, when the first layer had reached the gel state, the surface was manipulated slightly with a stick to produce an irregular surface with interesting light distributing characteristics. At this gel stage, a variety of foreign materials or objects may also be imbedded within the cells: metallic shapes, gears, industrial gadgets, electronic parts, colored cellophanes, or theatrical spotlight gelatins, and a variety of organic and inorganic materials, for example.

A second pour was made, filling the cells completely and covering the inserted objects. A piece of Mylar plastic was then placed over the surface of the resin to exclude the air (air inhibits complete curing) and to provide a smooth, glass-like surface. After the resin had hardened, the Mylar plastic sheets were peeled from both the front and back of the panel.

It should be noted that some dyes and pigments tend to either accelerate or retard the hardening of polyester; for example, certain reds and oranges retard polymerization, while blues and greens accelerate it. It is important, therefore, when employing colorants, to make an adjustment in the amount of catalyst used. Approximately six drops of MEK peroxide catalyst were used per ounce of polyester resin for the project shown here. This provided a pot life of about one hour.

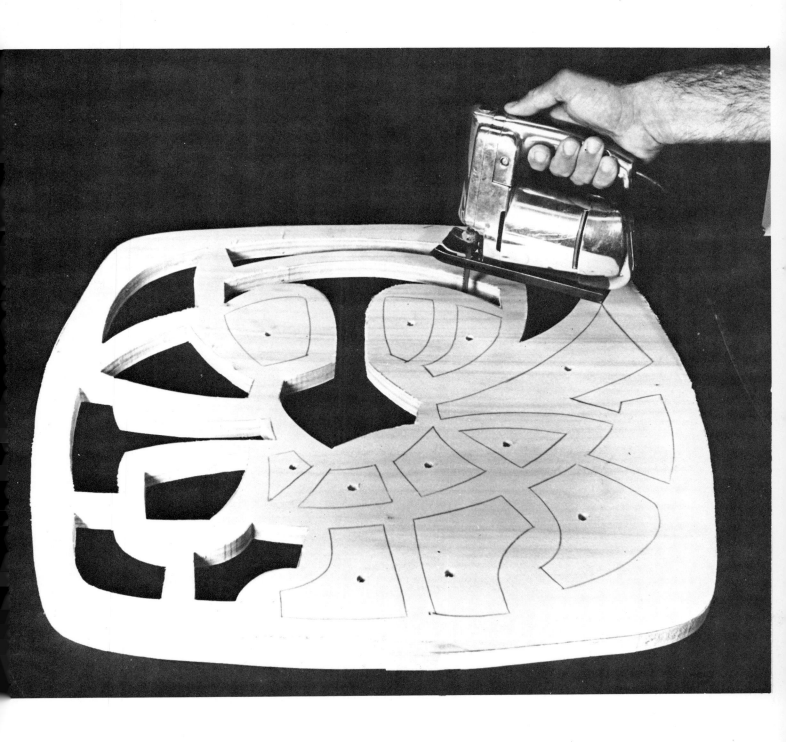

Step 1: ½″ plywood was cut with a sabre saw to create a panel with a cellular structure. It was sanded and then painted with an epoxy paint.

Step 2: (above) A sheet of Mylar is rubber cemented below the panel in preparation for pouring. Clear polyester casting resin is colored with polyester dyes, catalyzed, and poured into the cells of each panel. Two pours were employed to fill each cell, allowing the polyester to harden after the first pour before the second was made. Agitating the resin when it had reached a gelatin stage provided for more interesting light distributing qualities. A sheet of Mylar plastic was pressed to the top surface to exclude inhibiting air.

Completed Window Hanging (right) The Mylar plastic sheets are peeled away from both the front and back of the panel. Heavy screw eyes and rigid wire were used to suspend the window hanging. The panel measures 28″ square.

Nicholas Vergette, an American sculptor from Carbondale, Illinois, has developed an extremely interesting method of making translucent reliefs of polyester resin. His reliefs are multi-layered thicknesses of casting resin which include opaque, transparent, and translucent areas, with reflective mirrors imbedded within the resin to reflect light and color. Mr. Vergette uses the following method:

A large sheet of plate glass, used as the work surface, is supported on two trestles, or on a device—such as a light box—which will allow for viewing the work from underneath. Wooden strips are taped around the edges of the glass to act as a retaining wall, and the entire surface of the glass and wooden strips are coated with parting wax. Clear polyester casting resin is catalyzed (that is, catalyst is added) and poured into the frame to a depth of approximately ¼". After the resin has hardened, linear designs are painted on parts of the plastic with opaque oil or synthetic paints. Additional casting resin is colored with transparent dyes, then catalyzed, and poured over some areas of the design. The artist utilizes many colors and pours, constantly evaluating the cumulative effects from the underside of the plate glass.

Finally, pieces of mirror or polished metal are set at slight angles, face down over the design to reflect color and light through the relief. The panel is reinforced with a piece of fiberglass cloth laminated over the mirrors with polyester resin.

The panel is allowed to cure for three days before it is lifted from the glass and the wooden frame is removed. The underside of the panel, which now becomes the front, yields a variety of reflective qualities, changing as the spectator moves about in viewing the work. Mr. Vergette's use of a variety of brilliant colors and many layers of polyester resin develop an unusual depth and brilliance of color within his relief. The average size of his polyester panels is 35" x 24".

Relief panel (right) by Nicholas Vergette. 36" x 24". This panel was produced by brushing polyester resin over a clay mold. A sheet of fibreglass cloth, also impregnated with polyester, was brushed onto the clay. Then the panel was lifted from the mold. (See plate in color section.)

Step 1: (left) Photograph shows a craftsman in the process of chipping and faceting glass dalles for the purpose of creating a stained glass window of an epoxy-glass combination. Courtesy, Willet Studios, Philadelphia, Penn.

Step 2: (below) With the glass dalles chipped, faceted, and set in place over the full size working drawing, epoxy resin is catalyzed and poured around the glass to a thickness of about 1″. Courtesy, Willet Studios, Philadelphia, Penn.

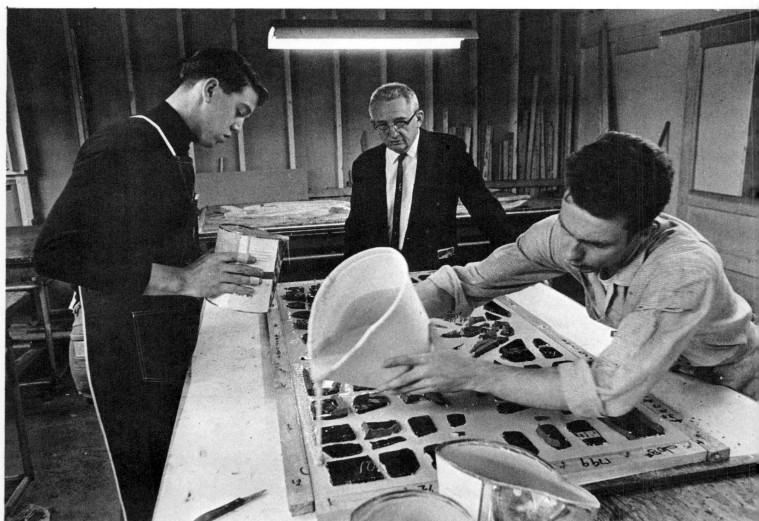

One of the most successful methods of creating architectural windows involves the combined use of stained glass dalles (pieces of colored glass) and epoxy resin. Transparent glass dalles are available in 1" x 8" x 8" squares in a variety of colors. Epoxy resin is poured around the dalles, serving as the "leading." Either small or large panels may be created by using this combination of materials. Epoxy resin is ideal for this use: it is lightweight, water repellent, and extremely strong, possessing excellent bonding characteristics and a negligible shrinking factor.

Working with glass-epoxy panels generally includes these basic steps:

(1) A full size drawing of the stained glass design is made on a sheet of heavy paper. This is then covered with a parting wax or film to prevent the plastic from sticking to the paper.

(2) A retaining frame is taped around the design and parting wax is applied to the inside edges of the frame.

(3) 1" glass dalles are chipped to fit individual sections of the design. The face of the glass is chipped, producing conchoidal fractures which create a jewel-like quality.

(4) The process of cutting and fitting the glass shapes to the drawn design is continued until the design is completed.

(5) Epoxy resin is catalyzed and poured between the glass dalles, filling the space to the level of the glass.

Epoxy resins are available in many colors and viscosities. The consistency of the epoxy resin required for this process should be similar to very thick pancake batter. Because these materials are toxic, use extreme care in handling them; adhere strictly to manufacturers' recommendations.

(6) The epoxy is allowed to harden, and the panel is then removed from the work surface.

Related to stained glass, in a sense, is another technique which exploits the light-transmitting qualities of acrylic. A channel can be incised on a sheet of transparent acrylic and this channel will literally conduct light from a source at the edge of the sheet.

The technique is simple. A router or some similar tool is used to incise the design on the surface of the sheet. The acrylic sheet is then polished and set into a box that contains the light source in the form of bulbs or tubes. The light flows into the channel and is "piped" across the sheet, illuminating the track left by the router.

Architectural panel (left) Willet Studios. Natural glass and epoxy are combined to create this stained glass panel. Epoxy plastic was poured around the glass, serving as the "leading." Waxed cardboard retaining rings were shaped and used for defining several areas, allowing for two levels of glass. Courtesy, Willet Studios, Philadelphia, Penn.

Stained glass-epoxy window (above) St. Luke's Church, Calgary, Alberta, Canada, by Robert Oldrich, 100' x 7'. The width of the opaque epoxy "leading" is varied, providing an effective contrast to the brilliantly colored glass. (See plate in color section.)

Piping light (above) through acrylic plastic sheet. Using a portable router, an incised design is created on the surface of a ¼" acrylic sheet. The design is cut to a depth of 1/16".

Lines in Space (right) by a design student, 16" x 16". The acrylic sheet is polished and set into a box containing a light source. A thin channel opening allows the light to enter the acrylic sheet from the bottom, and exit through the incised design, thus producing an illuminated linear design in space.

One method for making a lamp of thixotropic polyester involves the use of a plaster of Paris hump mold, which serves as a basic form over which a polyester shell is created. Many three dimensional, symmetrical molds may be easily made by using a metal template and simple jig—the shape of the template determining the shape of the mold.

In the process shown photographically here, a quarter-circle shape was cut into a metal template which was to serve as part of the jig for a half-sphere mold. This template was then fastened to a metal rod and set into a hole drilled into a sheet of ¾" plywood. Plaster of Paris was mixed with water to a thick consistency, and poured onto the central area of the plywood around the metal rod. As the plaster built up, the metal template was turned, and the half-sphere shape was evolved. When the form neared completion, thinner plaster was applied to obtain a smooth surface.

There are many other means of making hump molds. Plaster of Paris may be poured directly into large bowls or containers, or forms may be turned on lathes. A beach ball is a simple, yet effective, ready-made hump mold; thixotropic polyester resin may be troweled directly over the surface, allowed to set, and then the ball deflated and removed.

Before applying polyester resin over any pourous mold, the mold should be completely sealed and given a liberal application of wax and separating agent —also called parting agent—to prevent sticking. Plaster of Paris molds should first be allowed to dry thoroughly and then given three coats of lacquer to seal the porosity. Mold release wax is then applied liberally, allowed to dry, and polished. Finally, a coat of polyvinyl acetate (PVA) separating agent is carefully brushed over the wax surface to develop a thin parting film.

Thixotropic polyester resin—commercially available from most craft, boat, or plastic suppliers—is a thick, buttery substance that will cling even to vertical shapes without sagging. Chopped fibreglass strands should be mixed with the resin to impart greater strength. The polyester is catalyzed with MEK peroxide catalyst: from one to seven drops of catalyst to one ounce of resin, depending on temperature, thickness of cast, fillers, colors used, and age of the resin. An experiment conducted beforehand to ascertain proper resin-catalyst combinations, using the manufacturer's recommendations as a guide, may save headaches later. A spatula, trowel, or palette knife is used to apply the catalyzed resin to approximately ½" thick.

Before the resin has set, a variety of materials or objects may be pressed into the soft, thick surface. These objects become permanently integrated into the polyester shell after the resin has hardened. In making the lamp shown here, transparent, colored cubes—cast beforehand from polyethylene ice cube trays—were pressed into the soft resin. Two identical polyester shells were made and assembled to form a spherical-shaped red and blue lamp. Lamp fixtures were purchased from a local lamp shop.

Step 1: A metal template is cut to the shape of a quarter-circle, attached to a metal rod, and set into a ¾″ plywood base. This jig is turned, plaster of Paris is added, thus forming a half-sphere hump mold.

Step 2: The plaster form is sealed with three coats of lacquer, followed by an application of mold release wax, which is allowed to dry and is then polished. A coat of polyvinyl alcohol (PVA) is then brushed over the wax.

Step 3: Thixotropic polyester paste is mixed with chopped fibreglass strands to impart greater strength. The viscous mixture is then catalyzed with M.E.K. peroxide catalyst and troweled to the surface of the prepared plaster mold.

Step 4: Transparent cubes, casts from clear polyester resin using polyethylene ice cube trays as molds, are pressed into the soft resin before it sets. The cubes are placed in concentric circles, alternating in color as the work progresses from the top of the plaster mold downward.

Step 5: The completed half-sphere is easily removed from the plaster hump mold. Additional PVA parting agent is painted on the mold, and a second half-sphere is made in the same manner.

Spherical lamp (right) by Nicholas Roukes, 18″ in diameter. The two half-spheres are attached, using catalyzed thixotropic resin as the adhesive. The second half-sphere, used as the bottom section of the lamp, was created with a 6″ opening to allow for interior access. Lamp fixtures, such as socket assembly, threaded tubing with nuts and washers, electrical cord, and wall assembly were used to complete the lamp.

Galvanized stove pipe or furnace ducting are excellent armatures for making tube lamps. The ducting is first prepared by fitting wooden plugs on either end, with a bolt or metal rod running through the center so that the jig may rotate freely. A sheet of Mylar plastic is then taped to the surface of the pipe, acting as a "sleeve" for the easy removal of the fibreglass shells.

The hand lay-up process involves the use of polyester resin and fibreglass cloth over this jig. A coat of catalyzed polyester resin is painted over the tube, the jig being rotated slowly throughout the process to ensure the even application of the resin. While the resin is wet, a sheet of glass cloth is pressed into the surface. Additional resin is applied over the glass cloth, and compressed to the surface of the armature with a fibreglass roller. While the surface is still wet, a second sheet of fibreglass cloth is applied over the first one, creating a laminated fibreglass shell having a thickness of about ⅛″. The jig is continuously revolved while compressing the glass cloth with the roller.

When the polyester resin has set, preferably overnight, the fibreglass shell is removed from the jig, and work on another tube may commence. A total of four tubes were made for the lamps shown in this demonstration.

To decorate the surface of the tubular shells, many techniques involving plastics may be utilized. For example, glass or plastic shapes may be attached to the fibreglass tubes by first coating the shells with catalyzed thixotropic resin and then pressing the materials in to the pasty surface. Or, as we have shown in the photo sequence, the tubes may be divided into "cells" which are later filled with colored polyester resin. Cellular designs may be created by extruding thickened catalyzed resin from flexible catsup containers, or by attaching metal or flexible cord to the surface.

In making the tube lamps shown here, a soft leading, normally used for making stained glass windows, was easily shaped around the polyester tubes to create the cellular divisions. A soldering iron was used to join the lead pieces. In filling the cells, thixotropic polyester resin was colored with transparent dyes, catalyzed with MEK peroxide catalyst, and then applied with a palette knife. Many batches of resin were mixed with a variety of colors and the process was repeated until the surface of the lamp was covered. The colored paste resin had a translucent quality which dispersed light in an interesting manner.

A long incandescent light bulb was used for illuminating the lamps, 18″ in length, and orange, blue, and white in color.

Step 1: A simple jig for making tubular lamps is shown here. A galvanized metal stovepipe is fitted to a wooden cradle, allowing the armature to turn freely. Mylar plastic sheeting is taped to the pipe, in order to prevent the polyester resin from sticking to its surface, and to aid in the removal of the fibreglass tubes. Catalyzed polyester resin is applied to the tube with a roller, and a piece of fibreglass cloth pressed into the wet surface.

Step 2: A roller is used to apply additional resin and to compress the fibreglass cloth against the pipe armature. Two sheets of fibreglass cloth are laminated together in this fashion, creating a shell thickness of approximately ⅛″.

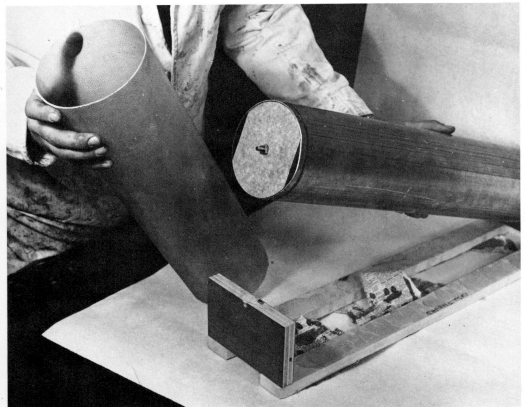

Step 3: Fibreglass tubes are readily removed from the jig, and are slipped out easily on the sleeve of Mylar plastic. Four tubes were constructed in this way in preparation for making an exterior lamp.

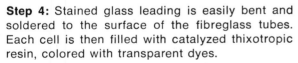

Step 4: Stained glass leading is easily bent and soldered to the surface of the fibreglass tubes. Each cell is then filled with catalyzed thixotropic resin, colored with transparent dyes.

Exterior lamps, 18″ long, polyester. These brightly colored lamps, made of fibreglassed polyester, display excellent weathering characteristics.

Clear acrylic domes, made by the blow-forming process, are available at electrical sign manufacturers, plastic fabricators, or skylight manufacturers. They are made by clamping a sheet of acrylic plastic between two sheets of wood, the top piece of wood having an opening cut to the size of the dome desired, and the lower one having a smaller opening for introducing air pressure. The frame containing the plastic is heated in an oven and removed when the acrylic has been softened. Air pressure is then introduced from the underside of the frame, blowing the dome to the desired height.

Acrylic domes are made for skylights, display cases, etc., and are fairly inexpensive to purchase. The artist may approach the fabricators directly for "seconds," or he may have them blown to his specifications.

Vinyl paints or lacquers are recommended for painting designs on acrylic domes. In making hard-edged designs, or for precise work, a liquid masking material, such as Gripmask, may be painted on the interior surface of the dome. This dries to form a thin, transparent blue film which is then cut with a sharp knife. Sections of the film are removed, exposing the plastic for spray painting.

For spraying transparent colors, Gripflex paints are recommended, and are available in many colors. Krylon spray paints may be used for spraying opaque designs.

After spraying the acrylic dome and allowing the paint to dry, the masking is peeled off. Additional coats of the liquid masking may then be applied, and more designs cut and spray painted, until the desired effect is created. Finally, an even application of opaque white Krylon lacquer is spray painted over the designs, serving as a light diffuser.

In completing the mushroom lamp shown in this demonstration, a small twenty watt incandescent light bulb was used for illumination. The lighting socket was mounted on a piece of ½" plywood, cut to a 20" circle, which served as the base for the lamp.

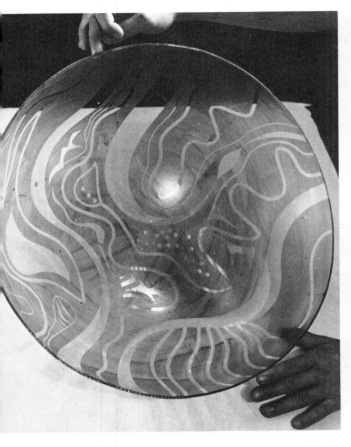 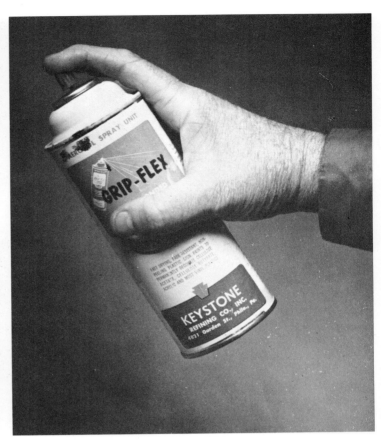

Step 1: Gripmask, a liquid masking material, is painted to the underside of a plastic dome. The material dries to form a film which is cut with an X-acto knife. Portions of the Gripmask film are peeled away, exposing the acrylic plastic for spray painting.

Step 2: Gripflex paint, a transparent plastic paint designed for decorating acrylic and other plastics, is sprayed over the dome. (Krylon spray paints were used in some areas for painting opaque designs.)

Step 4: The decorated plastic dome is fitted over a ½″ plywood base, drilled to allow for ventilation. A twenty watt incandescent bulb is used for illumination.

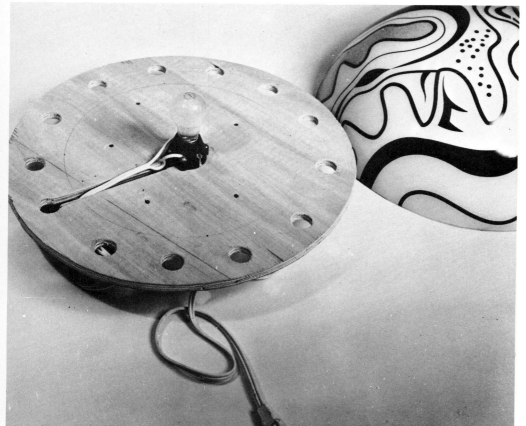

Step 3: After the colors have dried on the surface of the plastic, the Gripmask film is peeled away. The masking and painting operations are continued until desired effects are achieved. A final coat of opaque white lacquer is spray-painted over the design, acting as a light diffuser.

The completed lamp (right) This mushroom lamp measures 20″ in diameter and 9″ in height. It was designed in bright transparent yellow, green, and blue colors.

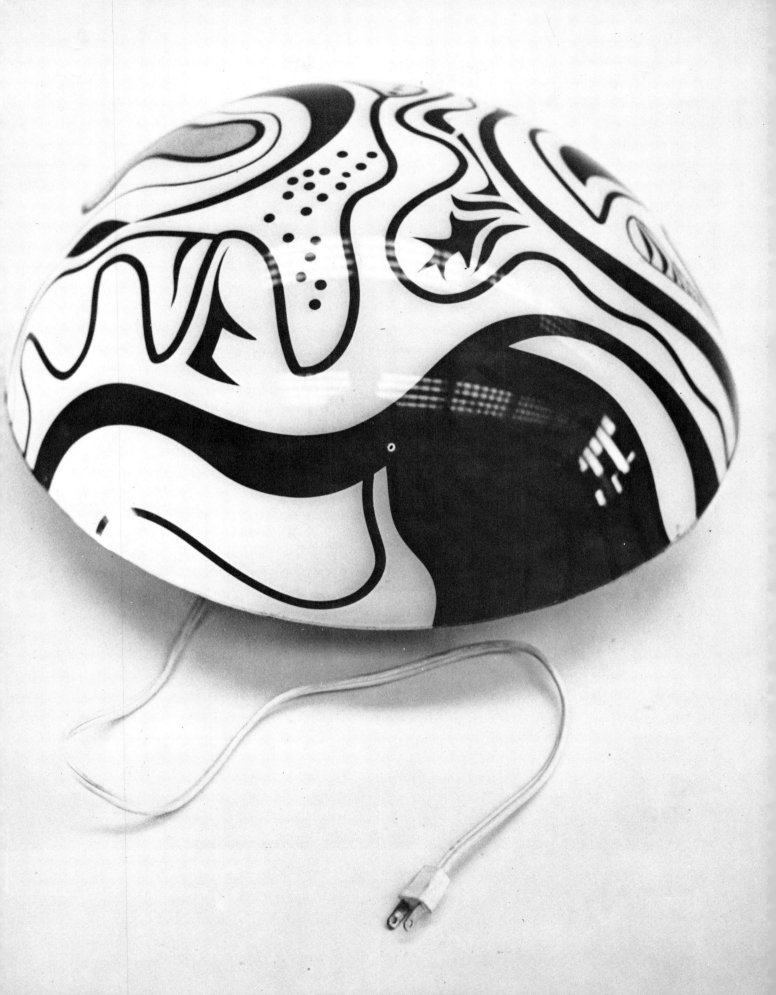

Table lamps (above) designed by Sergio Asti. Constructed in acrylic, produced by Kartell, Milan.

Table lamp (left) designed by Sergio Asti, Milan. Produced by Martinelli. Fibreglass cloth and polyester resin.

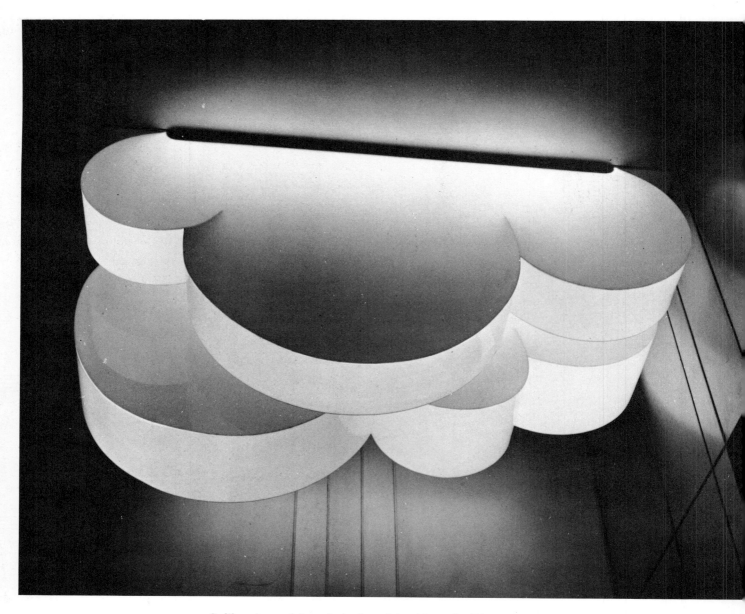

Ceiling lamp (above) designed by Marcello Pietrantoni, Milan, translucent white acrylic.

Hanging lamp (right) designed by Andreas Hansen, Le Klint, Denmark, polyvinyl chloride. These attractive Danish lamps are made by manually folding PVC plastic sheeting.

In addition to the uses already specified, plastic is a medium modern artists are using increasingly in sculpture and crafts. In this section, I intend to explore some of these uses: in sculpture, in collage, in paper maché, in vacuum forming, in making jewelry, constructions, and polyester inlay designs.

SCULPTURE AND CRAFTS

Expanded Plastics

Expanded polyurethane and polystyrene, commonly used for insulation purposes, are readily available from most building supply houses. These cellular plastics are lightweight, rigid slabs which have many applications within the realm of fine arts. Since the properties of these materials have been described in detail in my book *Sculpture in Plastics*, I shall concentrate on a few methods of using the materials which I believe the artist will find interesting to pursue.

The cellular plastics may be used in many ways, such as making non-permanent maquettes of lightweight sculpture, and as a mold material for subsequent casting in concrete, epoxy, or polyester resin.

The processes described in the first three projects of this section involve the use of commercially available cellular plastics. There are many artists working with foam-in-place methods for creating their own cellular plastics. However, these methods involve the use of highly toxic chemicals and are not recommended for general studio activity.

In this section, three methods of using cellular plastics are described:

(1) Making a relief panel of expanded polyurethane and polyester.

(2) Making a relief panel of expanded polystyrene and epoxy plastic.

(3) Making containers from expanded polystyrene and polyester.

Synthetic Media for Collage

Collage has been interpreted by many contemporary artists and critics as constituting, perhaps, the central force of the art of this century. More than ever before, artists and craftsmen are "assembling" their art, putting together a great variety of materials—creating work which ranges from flat, two dimensional forms, to three dimensional architectural-size sculpture.

The original collage technique, probably inspired by early folk art, involved cutting and pasting papers, and was utilized as an art form in the early 1900s by artists such as Braque and Picasso. The collages of Kurt Schwitters of about 1920 involved elements such as postage stamps, labels, bus transfers, theater ticket stubs, photographs, corrugated cardboard, cloth, nail heads, mirrors, and stenciled wood from packing crates. Even three dimensional forms, such as elements of furniture and heavy wire screen, were used to create some of his collage reliefs.

Later, artists extended the use of three dimensional collage. Artists such as Man Ray, Duchamp, Ernst, Breton, Miro, Cornell, Arman, Rauschenberg, Westerman, Kienholz, and Stankiewicz assembled a variety of three dimensional materials to produce sculptural collages, which were popularly called assemblages, or "combines." The collage idea soon expanded to include theater architecture, and even poetry and music. Today, collage includes the fourth dimensional realm as well. Many artists are busy at work, creating light kinetics, collage environments, and a variety of structured happenings.

In this section, for the purpose of explaining technique, we will deal with collage in a more restrictive manner, concentrating on the use of synthetic media for making collages of paper and mixed materials.

Paper Maché and Synthetic Media

The combined use of paper maché and plastic media offers two basic approaches for making craft articles or sculpture:

(1) Direct buildup of paper maché and acrylic medium over shapes or molds. In this instance, the final objects are created of paper which is reenforced by using the polymer binder, with subsequent decoration with acrylic paints or other media.

(2) Use of paper maché for making temporary armatures or cores. Here, the artist models paper maché forms and then applies thick, pasty mixes of polyester or epoxy resins over them. The paper maché forms are removed later, if desired.

Craft articles, as well as three dimensional reliefs and sculpture in the round may be realized with either method, possibilities which will also be explored in this section.

Jewelry from Plastics

Most of the plastic materials which I have described in this book and in my previous publication, *Sculpture in Plastics*, lend themselves to the art of making jewelry. Just a few of the methods and materials include the following:

(1) *Polyester Resin:* polyester resin may be cast into small molds and color or objects embedded within the castings.

(2) *Solid Acrylic:* acrylic sheets may be laminated together and then shaped with files, sandpapers, and buffs. Clear acrylic

tubes, rods, and blocks are also available commercially and lend themselves to jewelry projects.

(3) *Acrylic Polymer and Gel Mediums:* these may be used with paper maché for making "plastic maché" jewelry. Much harder forms are produced by the use of acrylic medium binders than would be obtained through the use of an ordinary wheat paste binder.

(4) *Expanded Polystyrene:* this combustible material may be used to create jewelry forms which are invested and then cast in hot metal. The expanded polystyrene volatizes immediately as the hot metal is poured into the mold.

(5) *Polystyrene Molding Pellets:* these thermoplastic pellets fuse together at about 330°F. in an ordinary kitchen oven, and may be arranged in many ways to create miniature sculptural forms.

(6) *Vinyls:* this is a very popular material for making colored mod jewelry. Thin vinyl sheets are available in many colors and metallic surfaces, and are easily cut with scissors.

(7) *Epoxy:* thick epoxy, filled with metal powders such as aluminum, bronze, or stainless steel, may be shaped like putty to develop miniature sculptural forms. Foreign objects, such as beads, glass, etc., may be pressed into the plastic before it hardens.

Audiohydro kinetic by Michael Hayden, anodized aluminum and acrylic with kinetic elements, courtesy Intersystems, Toronto, Ontario, Canada. Acrylic tubes are filled with red, orange, green, yellow, and blue fluorescent liquids. The construction includes two hydraulic and three pneumatic systems, a master timing device, and a twenty-five cent coin box. Two light systems are also integrated within the construction, one consisting of eight 4' ultra-violet lamps which are constantly on, and three 8' fluorescent colored tubes which are flashed for irregular durations by the master programmer. Sound is created by utilizing two tape recorders with continuous playback, channelled through twelve loudspeakers with a crossover network. Two tapes of different lengths are heard simultaneously, so that the music program is virtually never repeated.

Foam-Q (above) by Toshio Yoshida, acrylic and foam. Limpid, slow moving forms of foam, pumped in continuous action, are illuminated from within, creating a dramatic kinetic sculpture.

Upward Bound (right) by Michael Samford, polystyrene, Plexiglas, and lights, 24″ x 12″ x 12″. This sculpture is made by "thermo drop-forming," a technique whereby a sheet of polystyrene is clamped between two sheets of Masonite from which shapes have been cut out. The clamped panel is placed over a heater, and the polystyrene is softened until it sags through the open shapes in the Masonite. Two identical drop-formed elements are later laminated together, like parts of a clam, to create the three dimensional form.

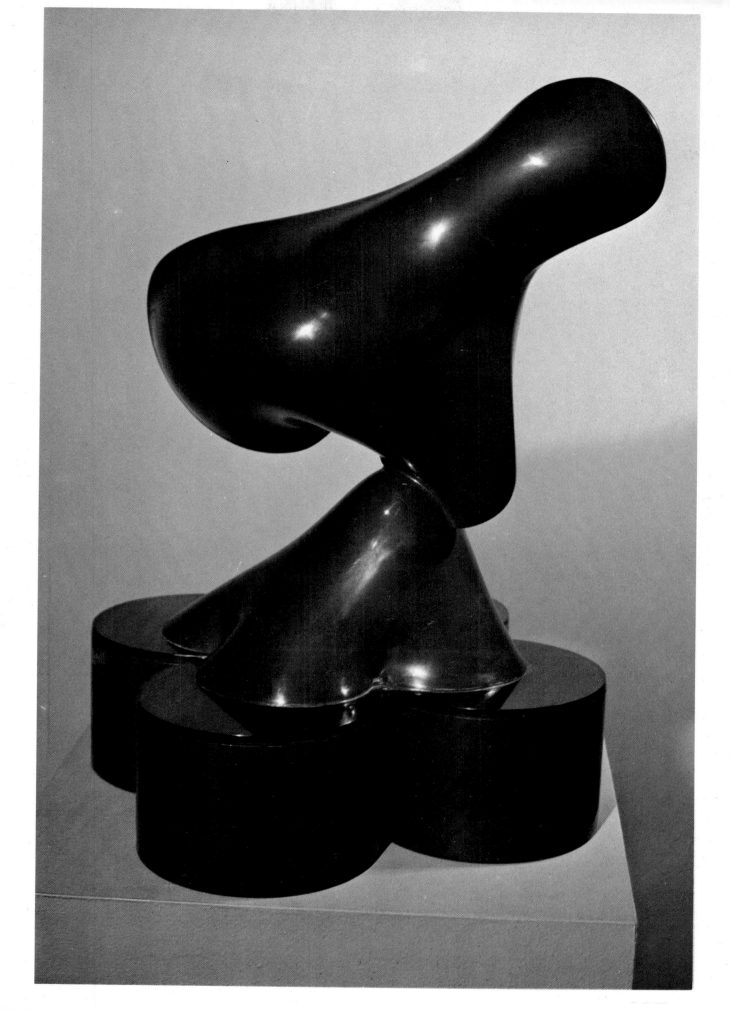

Wall hanging (left) by Ted Hallman, yarn and acrylic, 24″ x 5½″. Yarn is woven around painted acrylic shapes.

Decorative bird (above) by Nicholas Roukes, a coin bank, 10″. Brilliant red, yellow, and blue acrylic paint is used to decorate the surface of this paper mache form. Acrylic spray varnish is applied over the acrylic paint surface to obtain a shiny surface quality. (See Project 23.)

Acrylic constructions (above) by Dick Seeger. Colored acrylic sheet was cut and cemented together to form these luminous constructions.

Work (right) by K. Yamaguchi, 1.50 mm. This construction is made of transparent and translucent acrylic with interior illumination. Nagaoka Contemporary Art Museum collection, Japan.

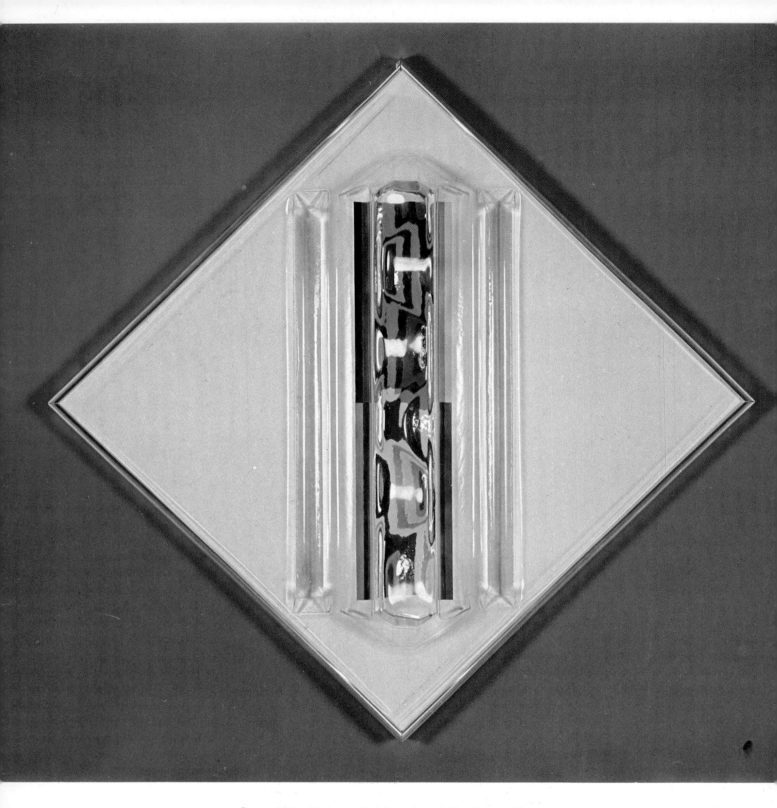

Optos 25 by Nicholas Roukes. A combination of silk screen print and vacuum formed plastic relief, this work is kinetic, using optics and color to produce a variety of optical effects as the spectator moves in front of it. Twenty-five multiples were created, each measuring 18″ x 18″. (See Project 8.)

Stained glass-epoxy window by Robert Oldrich, St. Luke's Church, Calgary, Alberta, Canada, 100' x 7'. Glass dalles are cut and faceted, and are enveloped in a matrix of epoxy resin. Gray in color, the epoxy resin matched the concrete structure of the church. Aggregate was grafted onto the wet epoxy just prior to hardening, in order to achieve a textural surface which integrated with the architectural design of the church.

Bird Forms (above) by Jean Varda, 32″ x 48″. Using acrylic polymer medium as the adhesive, a variety of textured fabrics of both natural and synthetic fibers were used to create this collage.

Colored reflecting panel (right) by Nicholas Vergette, 35″ x 24″. The polyester panel is developed by making many pours of colored polyester resin, with painted areas within the relief, and reflective mirrors set at angles on the backside to reflect color and light.

Interchanging Panels by Nicke Rosen, vacuum- and injection-formed plastic. A variety of colorful plastic shapes and background panels may be combined in many ways to create integrated linear patterns. Photo, Per Ostberg.

Relief panel by Nicholas Vergette. 36″ x 24″. This panel was created by brushing polyester resin over a clay mold. Pottery clay was used to create the basic matrix, and then coated with a layer of parting wax. Catalyzed polyester resin was brushed over the surface of the clay, and allowed to set. This was followed with the application of a sheet of fibreglass cloth, which was also impregnated with polyester. The panel was lifted from the mold, cleaned and polished. Bronze powder was used in the polyester as a filler, imparting a metallic quality to the final result.

Rings (above) by Siv Lagerström, acrylic plastic. A variety of ring forms can be cut out of acrylic sheet and polished, or acrylic monomer can be poured into molds— particularly for mass production—which makes possible the incorporation of liquid color in the casting.

Ice Flame (right) by Fred Dreher, clear acrylic, 8″. Such an intricate sculptural form can be created either by cutting and polishing a cast block of clear acrylic, or by pouring acrylic monomer into a carefully designed mold, after which the cast form is refined and polished.

Expanded polyurethane slabs have an average density of about two pounds per cubic foot, but they may be manufactured to many densities—up to thirty-two pounds per cubic foot for special orders. Unlike polystyrene, they are not dissolved or adversely affected by the corrosive action of the chemicals within polyester resin, and thus lend themselves to the technique of making molds for casting with polyester.

The photographic section in this project shows how a relief panel was created by carving a slab of expanded polyurethane, and then casting into it with thickened polyester resin. The slab was easily carved with a high speed Dremel tool, equipped with a round grinding burr. After the polyester had set within the polyurethane mold, the urethane was abraded away to reveal the casting. The rich cellular texture of the expanded polyurethane mold had been imparted to the polyester casting. If, however, a smooth finish were required in the casting, the urethane mold would be first coated with hot beeswax before pouring the polyester resin.

This technique, of course, is a waste mold process, and only a single casting may be made. The polyester resin is thickened by adding marble flour, or other fillers such as whiting, chopped or milled fibreglass fibers, silica, china clay, talc, or other such materials. It is desirable to add only a small amount of catalyst to the polyester in order to develop a longer pot life, and a cooler exothermic reaction. Too hot a mixture may heat the trapped gasses within the expanded polyurethane mold and distort its shape, resulting in a poor cast. In the photographs describing this process, one of the students from the author's class, John Charnetski, uses this process to develop a relief panel entitled *Constellation*. The panel measures 36″ square and is off-white in color.

Lost Dream, collograph by John Esler, 16″ x 17″. Acrylic paste extender was manipulated over a cardboard surface in creating a printing plate for this collograph. In some instances, the acrylic paste extender was allowed to dry for approximately one hour, sponged lightly, and several textural screens were pressed into the surface, thus transferring textures to the plate.

Step 1: (left) A high speed Dremel tool is used to grind a linear design into the soft surface of expanded polyurethane, which is to be used as a mold for casting with polyester. Ordinary kitchen knives and sandpaper are also used to shape the surface of the cellular plastic.

Step 2: (above) The completed mold is shown here, ready for casting with thickened polyester resin. No parting agent is used over the urethane plastic.

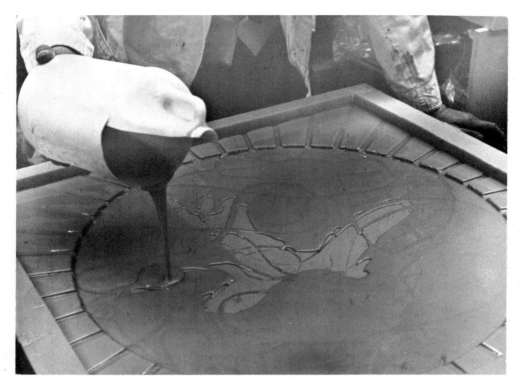

Step 3: A retaining frame made of polyurethane strips is placed around the mold in preparation for casting. Marble flour is added to polyester resin, equal parts by weight, and then catalyzed with M.E.K. peroxide. Approximately two drops of catalyst per ounce of thickened polyester are used, providing a pot life of about two hours. The thickened polyester resin is then poured into the polyurethane mold and allowed to set for twenty-four hours.

Step 4: Using a kitchen knife and wire brush, the polyurethane is removed from the casting.

Constellation by John Charnetski. Polyester, 36″ x 36″. The final cast possesses a rich surface texture, imparted from the cellular plastic mold.

A simple, yet effective method of making reliefs from polystyrene plastics (such as Styrofoam or DyPlast) is to use hot wire cutters, electric soldering guns or pencils, or wood burning tools to burn a design into the plastic and then to make an epoxy resin cast from the incised design. Electric soldering pencils work best, especially those equipped with a low-heat tip. Incised lines are burned into the soft cellular plastic almost effortlessly, and a variety of linear designs, shapes, and textures may be made with this tool. Allow proper ventilation for the dissipation of smoke from burning polystyrene; avoid inhaling the fumes.

Next, a plastic putty is selected which does not dissolve or adversely affect the expanded polystyrene; epoxy plastic resin satisfies this requirement. The resin is catalyzed and troweled over the surface of the design, building a slab thickness of about ½″. When the epoxy has set, the panel is reversed, and the expanded polystyrene dissolved with acetone, thus revealing the final relief.

Epoxy plastics are available in a wide range of colors, but the artist may choose to add special paste colorants to white epoxy resin for greater variation of color. The panel shown in the accompanying photograph was created by the author, using this technique. It measures 14″ square, and was made of black epoxy resin.

Step 1: (right) An electric soldering pencil is used to burn an incised design into the surface of expanded polystyrene.

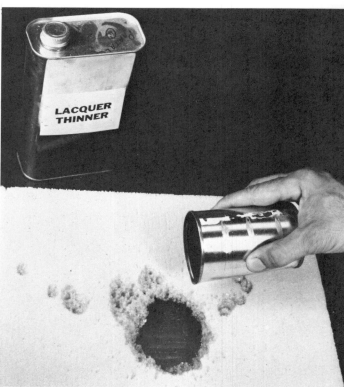

Step 2: Black epoxy plastic, used for automotive body repairs, is catalyzed with hardener and troweled over the surface of the expanded polystyrene to a thickness of approximately ½".

Step 3: The panel is reversed and lacquer thinner is poured over the expanded polystyrene, dissolving it readily.

Completed epoxy panel (right) by Nicholas Roukes, 14" square. The cellular texture of the expanded polystyrene has been transferred to the black epoxy panel, and incised lines now stand out in bold relief.

Hollow vases, or "polyester pots," are easily made by using expanded polystyrene as a temporary core. The cellular plastic is cut to the desired shape with a knife or hacksaw, or shaped to curvilinear forms using rasps, cheese graters, or sandpaper. Next, a protective coating of spackle, plaster, acrylic paste extender, or acrylic gesso is painted liberally on the entire surface and allowed to dry. Polyester is catalyzed and applied to the surface, building either a smooth or textured shell of about ⅜″ thickness. An opening is drilled into the hardened plastic shell, and lacquer thinner poured into the form. In this way, the expanded polystyrene is dissolved and poured out, thus creating the hollow form.

Thixotropic paste, polyesters, or epoxies may be used for this method. Color may be mixed into the resin before it is applied on the form, or the surface of the completed container may be painted later with either epoxy, polyester, or acrylic paint. Before the polyester or epoxy has hardened, materials or objects may be pressed into the surface, becoming integral parts of the shell after the plastic has set.

The following photographic sequence describes in detail the making of a "polyester pot." The completed pot measures 12″ in height.

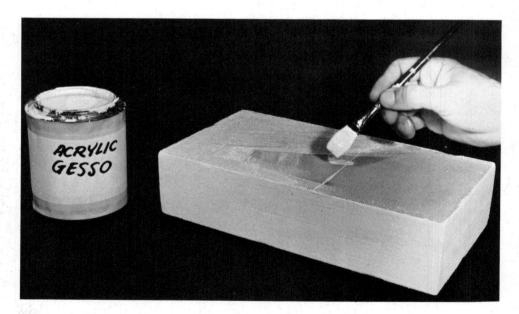

Step 1: (above) A block of Styrofoam (expanded polystyrene) is shaped and then painted with a heavy application of acrylic gesso. Plaster or acrylic paste extender may also be used to isolate the cellular plastic, thus preventing the application of polyester resin from dissolving it.

Step 2: (right) Clear polyester casting resin is catalyzed and poured over the surface of the form. Self-adhering weather stripping, attached to each side, keeps the liquid polyester from dripping over the edges.

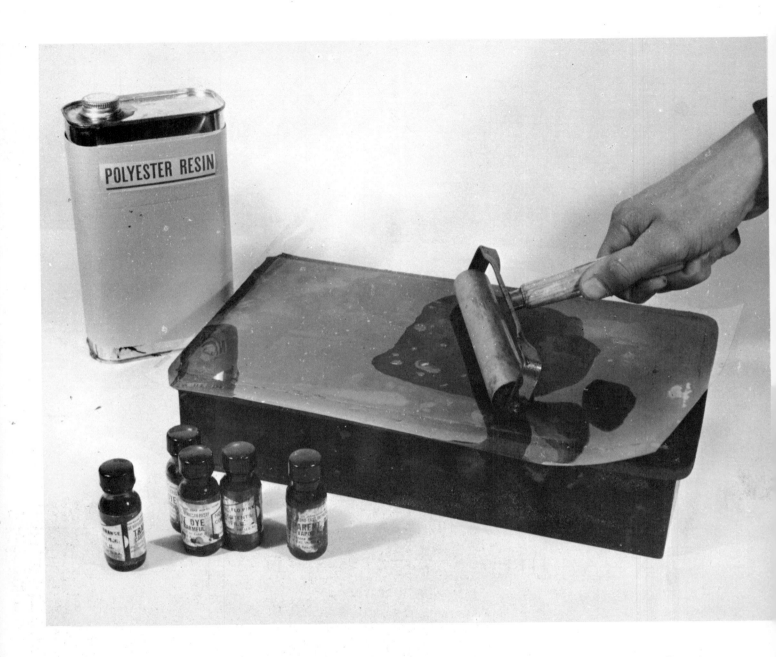

Step 3: The liquid polyester resin is spread evenly over the surface with a cardboard squeegee, and a piece of fibreglass cloth is pressed down over it. Additional batches of polyester resin are catalyzed and poured over the glasscloth. Subsequent batches include colored dyes and pigments. Metallic flakes, powders, and collage materials may also be incorporated into the design. To develop a glass-like surface and remove air bubbles, a sheet of Mylar plastic is placed over the top of the liquid resin and rolled from the center outwards. Each of the six sides are developed in this fashion, completely enveloping the cellular plastic with a polyester shell approximately ⅜″ thick.

Step 4: Holes are drilled into the polyester shell, allowing for openings at specific areas. Lacquer thinner is poured into the plastic container, dissolving the Styrofoam. This is then poured out, creating a completely hollow form.

Step 5: To complete the "polyester pot," three forms made of transparent polyester, are attached to the top with epoxy resin. (These forms were cast in spherical glass molds, shaped on a sanding belt, assembled, and drilled.)

Polyester pot (left) by Nicholas Roukes, 13″ x 7″ x 3″. Bright red, blue, yellow, and violet dyes, along with crimson metallic flakes are fused together to create an integral shell of polyester resin, approximately ⅜″ thick.

Polyester containers (right) by St. Maur, 15″ high, polyester-Styrofoam construction.

Plastic media, such as polyvinyl acetate (Elmer's glue), acrylic polymer and gel mediums, acrylic paste extenders, lacquers, polyesters, and epoxies may be used as adhesives for joining or adhering a variety of materials. The acrylic polymer medium is an excellent adhesive for papers and cloths. Where problems of water solubility are encountered, a non-water soluble adhesive medium, such as clear lacquer may be used. For assembling three dimensional objects or combining dissimilar materials, such as metal, glass, wood, ceramic, etc., a thick, strong adhesive such as epoxy is recommended.

The artist may want to introduce elements of photomontage into collage art. Photographic images may be transferred directly from magazine onto thin films of plastic. About three coats of acrylic polymer medium are brushed over a photograph, allowing each coat to dry before the next one is applied. When the final coat is dry, the photograph is held under a water tap adjusted for lukewarm water, and the image is carefully peeled away from the paper, much the same as removing a decal from its paper backing. The transparent photograph may then be applied to the collage, using acrylic polymer medium as the adhesive.

Materials such as polystyrene or other thermoplastic sheeting may be cut into a variety of shapes and forms which are overlapped and then heated in an ordinary kitchen oven to fuse the plastic. After the plastic collage has been removed from the oven—and while it is still warm—textural materials may be pressed into its surface to create rich patterns.

Transparent or opaque vinyl and acrylic are available in thin sheets suitable for making a variety of collages. Plastic contact papers with self-sticking adhesive backing, synthetic fabrics, and vinyl fabrics such as Uniroyal's Naugahyde offer additional possibilities as materials for making collages.

Producing Collages (left) Acrylic polymer or gel mediums are used as binders, combining torn papers, magazine cut-outs, textured cardboards, rope, etc. In collage-paintings, acrylic paints are also introduced, utilizing techniques such as glazing, scumbling, and overpainting.

Things Will Be Fine in '79 (below) by Faigee Hashman, detail of a collage painting, 28″ x 36″. A variety of torn papers and textural materials were used in creating this collage. Acrylic polymer medium was used as the binder. Acrylic paints were also introduced as the collage progressed, alternately glazing and scumbling over textural elements to produce rich textures and contrast.

Suburbia (left) by Faigee Hashman, detail of an acrylic collage, 24" x 36". Transparent tissues, textured papers, parts of a city map, and photographic cut-outs from magazines were combined on a surface of Masonite, primed with acrylic gesso. Acrylic polymer medium was used as the adhesive.

Meros (above) by Nicholas Roukes, plastic collage, 12" x 12". Polystyrene sheet was cut into a variety of shapes and overlapped to create the design. Work was arranged on a metal tray and then placed in a kitchen oven, fusing the thermoplastic to the desired degree. While the plastic was still warm, textural areas were created by pressing a metal grating into the soft surface.

Collage (left) by Jean Varda, 32″ x 48″. Acrylic polymer medium was used as an adhesive to attach many shapes cut from fabric to a plywood base.

Rigoletto (above) by Ken Morrow, acrylic collage, 48″ x 60″. Lavish amounts of white glue (polyvinyl acetate) were used to attach a variety of papers and fabrics to a Masonite panel. Acrylic color was applied over the collage, using scumbling and glazing techniques to develop rich surfaces. The collage was varnished with matt acrylic varnish.

The acrylic painting materials, such as polymer media, gesso, paste extenders, and gels, possess excellent adhesive qualities and may be used as effective binders for paper maché. Prepare the torn pieces of paper by soaking and softening them in a pail of water overnight. The water is drained prior to use. Dip the pieces of paper in polymer medium which has been diluted with water about 1:1, and then apply this to the molds or forms. Five to seven layers of paper maché are applied over the forms to build up the shell. When the shell has dried, a thick coat of acrylic paste extender may be applied, allowed to dry, and then sanded in order to obtain a smooth surface.

Shapes and molds for making paper maché shells may be created of practically any material: pottery or oil clay, plaster, wood, metal, stone, or from "ready-founds" scavenged from local wrecking yards. The acrylic paints are an ideal painting medium for decorating paper surfaces and can be applied by brushing, stippling, drybrushing, scumbling, or sponging.

The following photo sequence describes the use of paper maché and acrylic media for creating a whimsical bird bank.

Step 1: Plasticene clay is used to model the basic sculptural form. Since the surface is inherently oily and slick, no parting agent is required as a separator prior to the applications of paper maché.

Step 2: Seven layers of paper maché are built up over the clay mold, using polymer medium as the binder. Acrylic polymer medium is diluted with water at a proportion of 1:1. The paper maché is allowed to dry thoroughly for several days, creating a hard shell of approximately ⅛″ thick.

Step 3: The paper maché shell is sliced, with a sharp knife, into two sections and the clay form removed. The shell is then reassembled with additional laminations of paper strips saturated in polymer medium. For the final surface coating, a thick application of acrylic modeling paste is brushed over the hollow paper maché form, allowed to dry thoroughly, and then sanded in order to obtain a smooth surface.

Step 4: Acrylic paints are used to decorate the paper maché shell. Acrylic colors dry to a hard, waterproof state, and may be overpainted without danger of "picking up" previously applied color.

Decorative Bird, a coin bank, by Nicholas Roukes, approximately 10″ in length. (See plate in color section.)

Paper maché beasts (above) Paper maché and acrylic polymer medium. These delightful creatures were developed by saturating thin paper tissue in acrylic polymer medium and then by modeling this mixture over armatures constructed of wire and screen.

Torso (right) paper maché and photomontage, 16″ high. This sculpture was made of paper maché over clay. Acrylic polymer was used as the binder, producing a tough shell of approximately 3/16″ thick. When dry, the paper maché shell was cut from the clay and reassembled, like two halves of a clam, using additional paper maché strips and polymer medium. Magazine images were applied to the surface with acrylic gel medium.

Vacuum forming—the industrial process of thermoforming plastic sheeting—is attracting wide attention from contemporary artists. Used extensively in the sign-making industry, this process offers opportunities for making architectural reliefs, kinetic works, and molds for casting liquid polyester resin.

The fundamental process of vacuum forming is quite simple: a sheet of thermoplastic is clamped in a vacuum press, heat is applied to soften the plastic, and then the material is drawn either over a hump mold (drape molding) or into a female mold (straight vacuum forming). A vacuum is created by exhausting the air between the sheet and the mold, and normal atmospheric pressure then forces the softened plastic against the surface of the mold. After a brief cooling period, in which the plastic sheet hardens, reverse air pressure is applied to remove the part from the mold.

Vacuum forming machines are fairly expensive, and do not have to be part of every craftsman's studio equipment. In most metropolitan cities, there are sign manufacturers who do this for the artist at a reasonable cost.

Materials for making female molds include wood, metal, plaster, or a thermosetting plastic, such as epoxy or polyester. High strength plaster, such as U.S. Gypsum's Hydrocal B-II, is recommended for making female molds cast from clay reliefs.

In drape forming, practically any type of rigid material or relatively flat objects, such as automotive parts, gears, stones, metal shapes, etc., may be placed on a base and formed. A visit to the local junkyard should yield a gold mine of ready-founds for this purpose.

It is important to remember that exhaust ports, or vacuum holes should be drilled into the molds. These holes are drilled into the lower sections of the mold, or into the wooden base for an efficient vacuum and uniform "draw."

Typical thermoforming plastic sheeting includes butyrate, ABS plastics, polystyrene, acrylic, and vinyl. There are many more available in both sheet and roll form in a vast array of colors. They are available in varying thicknesses and in transparent, translucent, and opaque surfaces.

Designs may be painted or silkscreened on to the plastic prior to vacuum forming. If this technique is used, the craftsman should use a heat-resting paint, such as Nazdar's Plasti-Vac colors.

For making relief panels which are to include interior illumination, techniques similar to those employed by electric sign manufacturers may be used. The panels are vacuum formed of clear acrylic or butyrate plastic and then spray-painted from behind with transparent Grip-Flex paints, or similar transparent colors formulated for the sign-making industry. Following their application, an even spray of opaque white lacquer, such as Krylon's Spray Lacquer, is painted over them to provide a light diffusing effect.

In this section, a vacuum forming technique is used to create molds of polyethylene which are later used for casting jewelry.

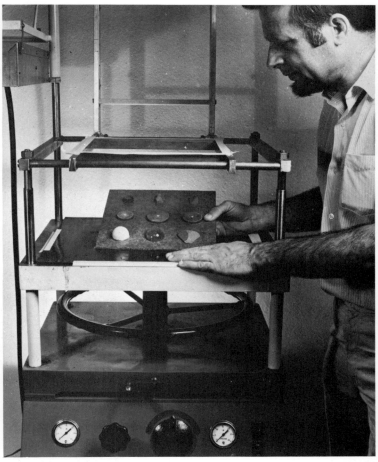

Step 1: A pattern for drape forming a thin polyethylene sheet is made of wooden and polyester shapes which are attached to a base sheet of Masonite with epoxy glue. Exhaust ports are drilled with a 1/16″ drill bit, through the Masonite base to provide an effective "draw."

Step 2: The wooden pattern is placed on the vacuum table in preparation for the thermoforming process. The press used in this demonstration was a Di-acro vacuum forming machine, capable of handling thermoplastic sheeting up to 18″ square.

Step 3: A sheet of 19" x 19" polyethylene plastic sheeting is clamped to the frame of the vacuum press. It is checked to insure that there are no air leaks as a result of uneven clamping.

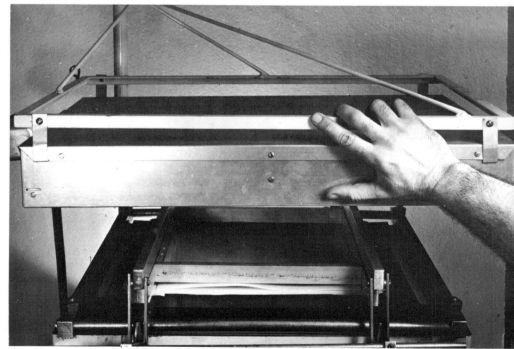

Step 4: The infra red heater is swung into position over the plastic, and allowed to heat the plastic for approximately three to five minutes, or until it develops an even soft, sagging quality.

Step 5: Vacuum is applied which allows normal atmospheric pressure to force the soft plastic sheeting down over the wooden pattern. The heater is then swung away from the press and the plastic is allowed to cool and harden before it is removed from the press. Applying reverse air pressure helps to release the plastic from the wooden pattern.

Step 6: Drape forming with vinyl sheeting and a wooden pattern. Thinner plastic was used, approximately 1/16″ thick, to insure reproduction of intricate design. In order to effect maximum "draw," exhaust ports were drilled through the Masonite base at 1″ intervals around the thicker ¾″ plywood.

The Completed Piece (left) by Nicholas Roukes.

Teabag (above) by Claes Oldenburg. Vacuum formed Plexiglas, cloth object and silk screen, 29″ x 39″.

In this project we will use a vacuum-formed mold for casting jewelry shapes. Molds for casting polyester resins may also be made from glass, ceramic, silicone rubber, vinyl, polypropylene, or porous materials, such as wood or plaster. Porous molds should be sealed with lacquer, given a coat of mold release wax, polished, and then given a final coat of polyvinyl parting agent (PVA).

The vacuum-formed molds used here were poured in two stages. First, they were half-filled with catalyzed polyester casting resin and allowed to gel. Cut-out shapes of colored cellophane and thin plastic sheet were then arranged over the gelled plastic. Materials such as dyes, pigments, crushed or pulverized stone or glass, mechanical parts, metallic powders, shavings, beads, foils, etc., were also imbedded within some of the molds. Finally, additional casting resin was poured over the designs, completely filling the molds.

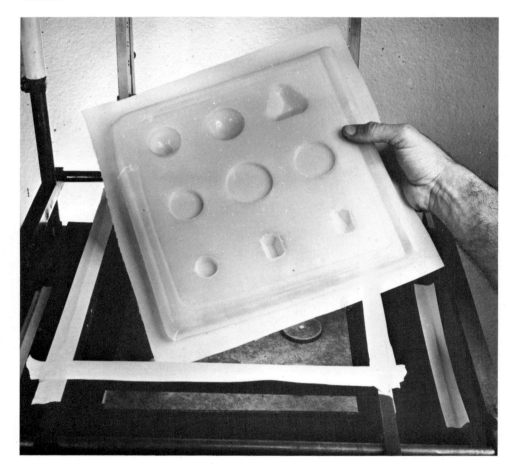

Step 1: Polyethylene molds were vacuum-formed for use with liquid polyester casting resin. (See Project 24.)

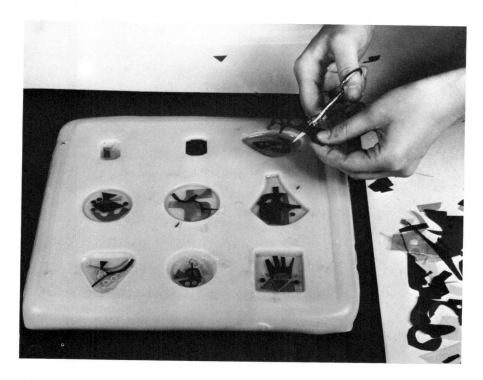

Step 2: Molds were half filled with catalyzed polyester casting resin and allowed to gel. Designs cut from transparent cellophanes and plastic sheets were arranged over the gelled plastic.

Step 3: The second pour of polyester casting resin fills the mold and imbeds the design within the plastic. The polyester is allowed to cure overnight.

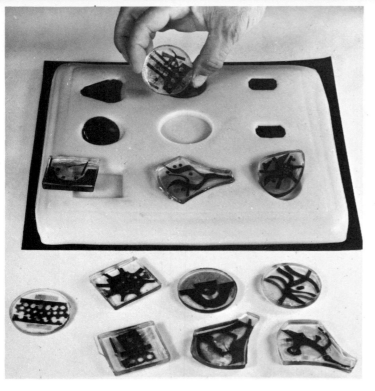

Step 4: (left) The solid, transparent forms are easily removed from the slightly flexible polyethylene mold. The mold is not adversely affected by the plastic resin, and may be used many times for casting.

The Completed Jewelry (below) Brilliant dyes, cellophanes, and reflective foils were incorporated within the polyester castings to create the bright, colorful forms.

Rings made from polyester resin cast into molds of RTV silicone rubber. Inclusions and painted designs within the plastic are optically magnified.

Solid acrylic sheets are available under such trade names as Plexiglas and Perspex, and come in thicknesses ranging from 3/64″ to 4″. Clear acrylic tubing is available in thicknesses of ¼″ to 18″, and acrylic rods in thicknesses of 1/6″ to 12″. Acrylics are soft materials and are easily cut, shaped, drilled, and polished with both hand and power tools. They may be softened in an oven at a temperature of about 275°F., and bent into dimensional shapes.

Acrylics may be sanded. Wet-dry aluminum oxide or garnet paper is recommended for best results in sanding acrylics. The #80-150 grit paper is normally used first, for preliminary sanding.

Acrylics may also be buffed and polished. Two muslin buffs, installed on an electric buffer, are used for these purposes. One buff is charged with white tripoli and used for preliminary buffing. The second is charged with white rouge and used for final polishing. Use care not to administer excessive pressure which could cause frictional heat and burning of the acrylic.

Use anti-static polishes. To eliminate static electricity and the accumulation of dust from the surfaces of acrylics, an anti-static wax should be applied periodically. The wax also helps to improve surface gloss.

For bonding acrylics, several materials are available. Solvents such as methylene dichloride and ethylene dichloride—or acrylic cement made by dissolving chips of acrylic plastic in one of these solvents—may be used to fuse acrylic surfaces together. Epoxy cements are used for joining acrylics to dissimilar materials, such as glass, metal, wood, or tile.

A note of caution: Methylene dichloride, ethylene dichloride, and cements containing these chemicals, are toxic and should be handled with care.

Acrylic Rings To make these rings, several brightly colored acrylic sheets measuring 1½″ x 1½″ x 3/16″, were laminated together to form a solid block. A solvent adhesive, made by dissolving scraps of acrylic plastic into metheylene dichloride, was then applied liberally to the acrylic sheets. The laminate was placed in a vise, set at moderate pressure, to compress the plastic sheets into an integral block. The plastic was drilled with a metal drill bit on a drill press, shaped on a belt sander, and polished with an electric buffer charged with tripoli and white rouge.

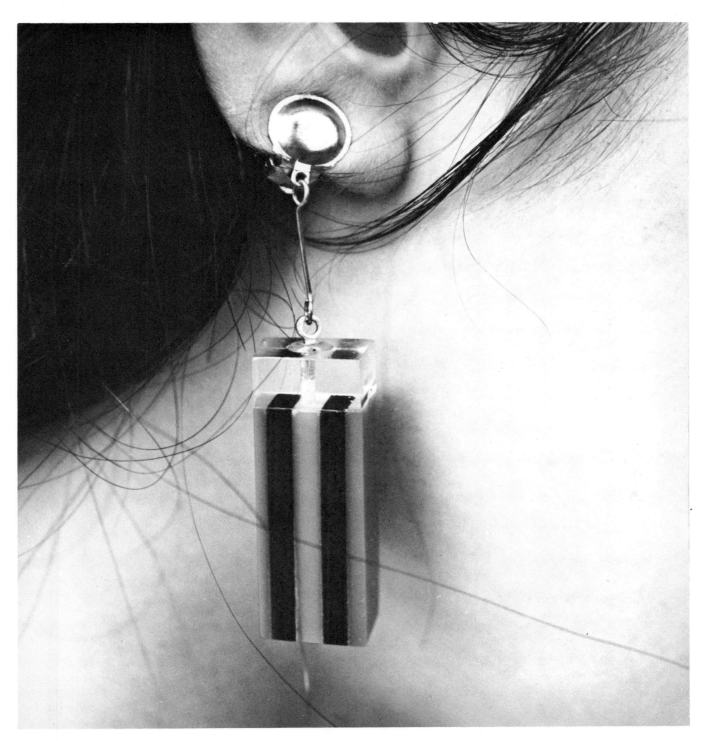

Earring, red, yellow, and clear acrylic. 3/16″ acrylic plastic was laminated together to produce this attractive jewelry.

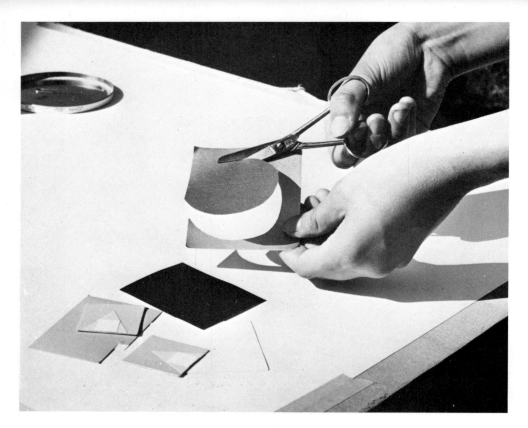

Cutting vinyl plastic sheet for making jewelry. This thin thermoplastic material is easily cut with household scissors. Vinyl is available in a wide range of colors, including metallic and fluorescent.

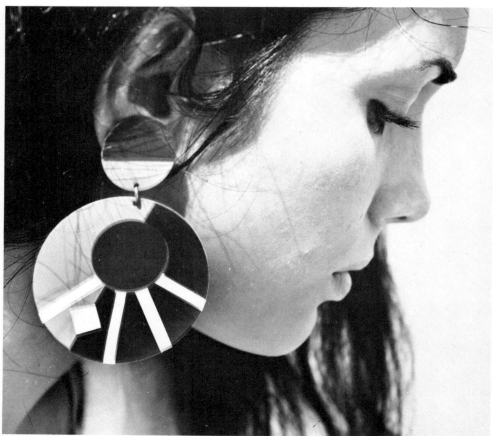

Vinyl plastic earring. Thin vinyl plastic sheets were cut with scissors to create these bright earrings. Shapes were glued together with vinyl cement. A leather punch was used to pierce holes in the plastic in order to join the two sections of the jewelry together.

Paper maché jewelry (right) Many layers of paper were laminated together with acrylic polymer medium to create this pendant. The design was created by applying designs which were cut from self-sticking vinyl plastic to the surface.

Here is a method of creating polyester inlay designs that may be used in many craft projects—wall reliefs, architectural room dividers, doors, coffee tables, lamp bases, or sculptural forms.

First, an electric router is used to channel a design, approximately ⅛" deep, into ¾" particle or composition board. The router blade cuts easily into the grainless surface of the compressed wood. The many cutting blades available for the router allow the artist to produce lines of varying widths.

Thicken polyester resin slightly by adding marble flour, talc, or other fillers, and then color this with polyester paste or dyes. The resulting thixotropic polyester mixture should have a consistency similar to that of heavy pancake batter. It is then catalyzed with MEK peroxide and poured into a plastic squeeze bottle. The polyester is extruded from the plastic containers into the channels of the design. The channels are generously filled with the plastic resin and allowed to cure overnight.

Finally, the panel is sanded with a portable electric sander until all portions of the polyester design are flush with the wooden surface. As a final finish, satin matte urethane varnish is brushed over the entire surface of the panel.

The following photo sequence shows the creation of a polyester inlay panel, designed to serve as a top for a coffee table.

Step 1: An electric router is used to incise a design ⅛" deep on particle board.

Step 2: Polyester resin, thickened with marble flour and catalyzed with MEK peroxide catalyst, is extruded from a plastic squeeze bottle, filling the channels of the incised design.

Step 3: Raised portions of the polyester design are sanded flush to the surface of the wooden panel.

Completed Panel Satin matt urethane varnish is brushed over the surface as a final finish. The panel, 24″ x 56″, serves as a top for a coffee table.

Note that some manufacturers may sell only in large quantities. Write them for the names of local distributors, or check the local classified telephone directory under Plastics or Boat Equipment and Supplies.

Acrylic Monomers
DuPont Company, Plastics Department, Wilmington, Delaware.

Acrylic Scratch Removal Kit (polysand)
Micro-Surface Finishing Products, Inc., Box 249, Burlington, Iowa 52601.

Acrylic Sheet
Altuglas, 40 Avenue Kleber, Paris, France.
Cadillac Plastic, 148 Parkway, Kalamazoo, Michigan.
Cast Optics Corporation, 1966 S. Newman Street, Hackensack, New Jersey 07602.
Imperial Chemicals Industries, Ltd., Plastics Division, Welwyn Garden City, Herts, England (Perspex).
Plastic Sales, Inc., 863 Folsom Street, San Francisco, California.
Rohm and Haas Company, Independence Mall West, Philadelphia, Pennsylvania, 19105 (Plexiglas).
Shinkolite, Mitsubishi Rayon Company, Ltd., No. 8, 2-Chome, Kyobashi, Chuo-ku, Tokyo, Japan.

Acrylic Water Wax Extender
Durable Arts, Box 2413, San Raphael, California 94901.

Anti-static Solutions
Chemical Development Company, Danvers, Massachusetts (Anstac 2M).
Playtime Products, Inc., Functional Products Division, 442 N. Detroit Street, Warsaw, Indiana (Negastate 102 aerosol spray).

Catalysts
Apogee Chemical, Inc., DeCarlo Avenue, Richmond, California.
McKesson & Robbins, Chemical Department, 155 East 44th Street, New York, New York 10017.
Wallace & Tiernan, Inc., Lucidol Division, 1740 Military Road, Buffalo, New York 14240.

Cements (plastic)
Cadillac Plastic & Chemical Company, 15111 Second Avenue, Detroit, Michigan (Cements 1-B, 11, PS-18).
Schwartz Chemical Company, Inc., 50-01 Second Street, Long Island City, New York 11101 (Rez-N-Dye).

Colorants for Plastics
American Hoechst Corporation, Carbic Color Division, Mountainside, New Jersey, or 129 Quidnick Street, Coventry, Rhode Island 02816.
Ferro Corporation, Color Division, Cleveland, Ohio 44105.
Patent Chemical, Inc., 335 McLean Blvd., Paterson, New Jersey.

Pfizer Company, Inc., 235 E. 42nd Street, New York, New York 10017.
Plastic Molders Supply Company, Inc., 75 S. Avenue, Fanwood, New Jersey.
Plastics Color, Division of Crompton & Knowles Corporation, 22 Commerce Street, Chatham, New Jersey 07928.
Ridgway Color and Chemical Company, 75 Front Street, Ridgway, Pennsylvania 15853.

Concrete Plastic Additives
W. R. Grace Company, Dewey and Almy Chemical Division, Cambridge, Massachusetts.

Disintegrated Metals (nickel, tin, aluminum, copper, bronze, lead, stainless steel)
Metals Disintegrating Corporation, P.O. Box 290, Elizabeth, New Jersey.
U.S. Bronze Powders, Inc., Route 202, Flemington, New Jersey 08822.

Fibreglass Cloth
Burlington Glass Fabrics, 1450 Broadway, New York, New York 10018.
Ferro Corporation, Fibreglass Division, 200 Fibreglass Road, Nashville, Tennessee 37211.
Gustin-Bacon Manufacturing Company, 210 W. 10th Street, Kansas City, Missouri.
Pittsburgh Plate Glass Company, Fibreglass Division, One Gateway Center, Pittsburgh, Pennsylvania 15222.
Western Fibrous Glass Products, 739 Bryant Street, San Francisco, California.

Fibreglass Laminating Equipment
Peterson Products, 1325 Old Country Road, Belmont, California.

Fillers
Cabot Corporation, 125 High Street, Boston, Massachusetts (Cab-O-Sil).
Georgia Kaolin Company, 41 Parker Road, Elizabeth, New Jersey (clays).
National Gypsum Company, Buffalo, New York 14225 (limestone).
Plymouth Fibers Company, Inc., Traffic and Palmetto Streets, Brooklyn, New York 11227 (cotton flock).
Powhatan Mining Company, 6723 Windsor Mill Road, Baltimore, Maryland 21207 (asbestos).
Wood Flour, Inc., 3 Howard Street, Winchester, New Hampshire 03470.

Gypsum Plasters
U.S. Gypsum Company, 300 West Adams Street, Chicago, Illinois (Hydrocal A-11, B-11, Hydrocal white, Hydrostone, Ultracal).

Hot-Wire Cutters
Dura-Tech Corporation, 1555 N.W. First Avenue, Boca Raton, Florida.

Jewelry Supplies, Findings, Buffers, Torches

Allcraft Tool and Supply Company, 215 Park Avenue, Hicksville, New York 11801.

Lamp Parts

Lamp Products, P.O. Box 34, Elma, New York.

Masking Compounds

Spraylat Corporation, 1 Park Avenue, New York, New York 10016 (Spraylat).

Masking Papers

Permacel, U.S. Highway #1, New Brunswick, New Jersey (Permacel 01 pressure sensitive paper).

Mold Releases

Axel Plastics, 41-14 29th Street, Long Island City, New York 11101.

Carlisle Chemical Works, Inc., 1801 West Street, Reading, Ohio 45215 (mold release waxes).

Dow Chemical Products Division, Midland, Michigan.

Ellen Products Company, Inc., 131 S. Liberty Drive, Stony Point, New York (silicone mold releases).

Mitchell Rand Manufacturing Corporation, Hillburn, New York.

Specialty Products Corporation, 15 Exchange Place, Jersey City, New Jersey 07302.

Molds

Devcon Corporation, Danvers, Massachusetts (Flexane—liquid urethane).

Dow Chemical Company, Midland, Michigan (Silastic RTV).

General Fabricators, Van Nuys, California (Plastiflex).

Smooth-on Manufacturing Company, 572 Communipaw Avenue, Jersey City, New Jersey (Smooth-on PMC-703).

U.S. Rubber Company, 1230 Sixth Avenue, New York, New York (mold materials).

Muiti-lensed Plastic Sheeting

Edmund Scientific Company, 101 E. Gloucester Pike, Barrington, New Jersey 08007 (op & moire).

Ovens

Electric Hotpack Company, 5083 Cottman Street, Philadelphia, Pennsylvania 19135.

Paints for Plastic (acrylic artists' colors)

Bocour Artists Colors, Inc., 552 West 52nd Street, New York, New York 10019.

California Products Corporation, New Masters Fine Arts Division, 169 Waverly Street, Cambridge, Massachusetts 02139.

Dana Colors, Inc., 1833 Egbert Avenue, San Francisco, California 94124.

M. Grumbacher, Inc., 460 West 34th Street, New York, New York 10001.

Morilla Company, Inc., 43-01 Street, Long Island City, New York 11101.

Permanent Pigments, Inc., 27000 Highland Avenue, Cincinnati, Ohio 45212.

Politec Company, Tigre 24, Mexico 12, D.F., or 425 14th Street, San Francisco, California 94103.

Reeves and Sons, Ltd., Lincoln Road, Enfield, Middlesex, England, or 16 Apex Road, Toronto, Canada.

George Rowney & Company, Ltd., 10/11 Percy Street, London, W1, England.

Shiva Artists Colors, Shiva-Rhodes Building, 10th and Monroe Streets, Paducah, Kentucky 42001.

F. Weber Company, 1220 Buttonwood Street, Philadelphia, Pennsylvania 19123.

Paints for Plastic (industrial)

Glidden Acrylic Sign Finishes, Glidden Company, 11001 Madison Avenue, Cleveland, Ohio.

Keystone Refining Company, Inc., 4821-31 Garden Street, Philadelphia, Pennsylvania 19137 (Grip-Flex).

Parting Agents

Costa Chemicals, Laguna Beach, California (Formula Five).

Specialty Products Company, 15 Exchange Place, Jersey City, New York 07302.

Parting Film (silicone release paper)

Dow Corning, Midland, Michigan.

Plastic Film

Flex-o-Glass, Inc., 1100 N. Cicero Avenue, Chicago, Illinois 60651.

Plastic Impregnating Materials

Cal Resin, 14812 Raymer Street, Van Nuys, California (industrial coatings and resins).

Furane Plastics, 4516 Brazil Street, Los Angeles, California 90039 (Plaspreg).

Plastic Molding Crystals

California Crafts Supply, Box 154, Buena Park, California.

Plastic Polishes and Polishing Compounds

Costa Chemicals, Laguna Beach, California (Formula 5 Clean and Glaze Wax).

Goodison Manufacturing Company, Box 128, Rochester, Michigan (Triple A Buffing Compound).

The Lea Manufacturing Company, 239 East Aurora Street, Waterbury, Connecticut, 06720 (Learock 765 for cutdown, Learock 884 for coloring, Learock 339 for high coloring).

Mirror Bright Polish Company, Pasadena, California.

Plastic Putties

Boyle-Midway Household Products, South Avenue and Hale Street, Cranford, New Jersey (Plastic Wood).

Devcon Corporation, Danvers, Massachusetts (Plastic Steel).

Sculpmetal Company, 701 Investment Building, Pittsburgh, Pennsylvania 15222, (Sculpmetal).

Woodhill Chemical Company, 18731 Cranwood Parkway, P.O. Box 7183, Cleveland, Ohio 44128 (Duro-Plastic Aluminum, Liquid Steel, Gook).

Plastic Sheets, Rods, Tubes

Commercial Plastics & Supply Corporation, 630 Broadway, New York, New York 10012.

Polyester and Epoxy Resins

Reichhold Chemicals, Inc., RCI Building, White Plains, New York.

Shell Chemical Company, Plastics & Resins Division, 110 West 51st Street, New York, New York 10020.

Taylor & Art, Inc., 1710 East 12th Street, Oakland, California 94606.

Polystyrene

Sinclair-Koppers Company, Koppers Building, Pittsburgh, Pennsylvania 15219.

Polystyrene Pellets

Shell Oil Company, Plastics Division, 110 West 51st Street, New York, New York, 10020.

Printing Inks

California Ink Company, 501 - 15th Street, San Francisco, California.

Craftools, Inc., 396 Broadway, New York, New York.

Flax Artist Supplies, 10852 Lindbrook Drive, Los Angeles, California.

Hunt Manufacturing Company, Box 560, Camden, N.J.

Inter-Chemical Printing Corporation, 16th and Willow, Oakland, California.

Leber Ink Company, Box 606, Tukwila, Washington.

S. Wolfs & Son, 771 - 9th Avenue, New York, New York.

Printing Papers

Aiko's, 714 N. Wabash, Chicago, Illinois.

Zellerbach Paper Company, 245 S. Spruce Street, South San Francisco, California.

Printing Presses

American Graphic Arts, Inc., 628-642 West 15th Street, New York, New York.

Charles S. Brand, 82 East 10th Street, New York, New York 10003.

Craftools, Inc., 396 Broadway, New York, New York.

Edward Dickerson, 2034 N. Mohawk St., Chicago, Ill.

Rembrandt Graphic Arts Company, Stockton, N.J.

Printing Presses (blankets for printing presses)

Graphic Chemical & Ink Company, Inc., P.O. Box 27, Villa Park, Illinois.

Pacific States Felt & Manufacturing Company, 843 Howard Street, San Francisco, California.

Printing Rollers, Brayers

California Ink Company, 501 - 15th Street, San Francisco, California.

Craftools, Inc., 396 Broadway, New York, New York.

Graphic Chemical and Ink Company, Inc., P.O. Box 27, Villa Park, Illinois.

Printing Tarlatans

Beckman & Company, 120 Baxter Street, New York, N.Y.

Printing Tools

Craftools, Inc., 396 Broadway, New York, New York.

Rembrandt Graphic Arts Company, Inc., Stockton, New Jersey.

F. Weber, 1220 Buttonwood Street, Philadelphia, Penn.

Release Agents See Parting Agents

Router Bits

American Rotary Tool Company, 44 Whitehall Street, New York, New York 10004.

Atrax Company, 240 Day Street, Newington, Conn.

Edstrom-Carlson & Company, 1400 Railroad Avenue, Rockford, Illinois.

Oceana Tool Manufacturing Company, Inc., 4143 Glencoe Avenue, Venice, California.

Routing Equipment

Rockwell Manufacturing Company, Delta Power Tool Division, 400 N. Lexington Avenue, Pittsburgh, Pennsylvania 15208.

Porter-Cable Machine Company, 700 Marcellus Street, Syracuse, New York 13204.

Stanley Electric Tools, Division of The Stanley Works, New Britain, Connecticut.

Saw Blades (carbide tipped)

Forrest Manufacturing Company, 240 Highway 11, Rutherford, New Jersey, or 231 Highway 17, Rutherford, New Jersey.

Lafayette Saw & Knife Company, 87 Guernsey, Brooklyn, New York 11222.

Lemmon & Snoap, 2618 Thornwood S.W., Grand Rapids, Michigan.

Radial Cutter Manufacturing Company, 831 Bond Street, Elizabeth, New Jersey.

Saw Blades (veneer)

Acme-Detroit Saw Corporation, 528 Fort Street, East Detroit, Michigan.

Atkins Saw Division, Borg-Warner Corporation, 402 S. Illinois Street, Indianapolis, Indiana.

Simonds Saw & Steel Company, Fitchburg, Mass.

Sculpture Supplies

Sculpture Associates, 101 St. Mark's Place, New York 9, New York.

Silk Screen Supplies

Advance Process Supplies Company, 400 N. Noble, Chicago, Illinois 60622.

Naz-Dar Company, 1087 North Branch Chicago, Illinois.

Ulano Graphic Arts Supplies, Inc., 610 Dean Street, Brooklyn, New York 11238.

Stained Glass

Whittemore-Durgin, Box K2065, Hanover, Massachusetts 02339.

Strip Heater

Electric Hotpack Company, Inc., 5083 Cottman Street, Philadelphia, Pennsylvania 19135.

Urethane (rigid)

Aircraft Specialties Company, Inc., Foam Division, 37 West John Street, Hicksville, New York (expanded cellulose acetate, rigid cellular plastic).

Allied Chemical Company, Barrett Division, 40 Rector Street, New York, New York 10006.

Nopco Chemical Company, 60 Park Place, Newark, New Jersey (pour-in-place liquids).

The Upjohn Company, 555 Alaska Avenue, Torrance, California 90503.

Vacuum Forming Machines

O'Neil-Irwin Manufacturing Company, Lake City, Minnesota (Di-Acro Plastic Press).

Spencer-Lemaire Industries, Ltd., Edmonton, Alberta, Canada.

Vinyl (sprayable)

R. M. Hollingshead Corporation, Camden, New Jersey (Cocoon).

INDEX